CW01498744

The Road
of the
Mountaineers

Die Strasse der
Gebirgsjäger

Lisa Frei

Die Strasse der Gebirgsjäger

© Copyright 2015 Elisabeth Frei

https://lisafrei.wordpress.com/

All rights reserved.
No part of this publication may be reproduced, stored in a retrieval system, or transmitted, in any form or by any means, electronic, mechanical, photocopying, recording or otherwise, without the prior written permission of the publisher.

Cover Photograph of Fritz Reinmüller

ISBN: 978-1-910853-01-6

Published by:

Lioness Publishing

Highlands, Wharncliffe Road, Ilkeston, Derbyshire, DE7 5GF, England

LionessPublishing.com

Die Strasse der Gebirgsjäger

Acknowledgements

This book has been a long time in coming. Already in 1977, the thought to write this book was put into my head by my children Michael and Angela. Michael had just turned 13 years and Angela 10.

I was preparing our evening meal in the kitchen at our home, in Norfolk. They were both helping me, when Michael started asking me about certain things from WW2, as he knew that back then I lived in Bavaria, in the village where I was born, near Munich. They were just learning something about this period at school. I answered all his questions and they both listened attentively. I was surprised to realise how interested both of them were. Then when I quite casually mentioned:

"And when your uncle Toni came home from his imprisonment in France..."

Michael with astonishment asked me: "Do you mean to say that my uncle was a prisoner of war? Wow!"

Now it was my turn to be surprised as I said: "Well, yes. Didn't you know that?"

"No", he said, "That never came up in any conversation, not even when I was on holiday with them. I knew that both uncle Toni and uncle Shorsh had been soldiers in WW2 and I did know that uncle Toni was in Finland and uncle Shorsh in Russia, but that's about it."

Angela asked me: "Mama, were you a little girl then?" She seemed to find it difficult to understand that her mother was once a little girl.

Through this conversation with my children I knew that I had to write this book. How else would they ever know anything about my history and consequently also theirs?

Thank you to all the people who so generously helped me with information and dates.

My very special thanks go to my son Michael and my daughter Angela. Throughout writing this book they gave me their support and advice in constructing this book in a chronological order. Once I had finished the work of writing they generously spent time in editing and helping me choose the photos. However many hours they spent on my book, they were still ready to give me more help whenever it was needed.

I also want to thank my daughter Angela for her enthusiasm and encouragement while I was writing. Although living in Geneva, Switzerland, she never stopped giving me her support while telephoning me very frequently, and asking about the progress I was making. She never stopped telling me how important this piece of work was. She actually told me that she thought that they are very fortunate that I have undertaken to write my family's history from before, during and after WW2. Her words: "Otherwise we would never have known!"

Also my special thanks go to my distant cousins Maria and Therese Riesinger, who were history teachers for 35 years until their retirement. Therese was the author of the book "The Chronicle of Ismaning", which she gave to the local council in the year 2004. I was fortunate enough to be presented with a copy by some of my school friends. When I asked Therese and her sister Maria, whether I could possibly use some of her research for the book I was intending to write, I was surprised at their enthusiasm and especially at their warmth. They both agreed, and even said that it would be an honour to use some of the research in my book, in England.

To my great sadness Therese will never read my book as she died in 2010, at the age of 83. When I expressed my regret to Maria, her sister, she said: "Don't you worry, Resi will know, and she will send you her blessing."

I am quite sure of that.

My special thanks also go to Sister M. Consolata Neumann, at the Mother Convent Unterer Anger, in Munich. Sister M. Consolata is the archivist at the Mother Convent and very kindly made all the relevant documentation available to me.

In 2010, I spent an afternoon in the library of the Convent looking through the documents and at the same time enjoying the beautiful view of the serene and peaceful garden. After an hour had elapsed and I had concluded my research, Sister Consolata joined me and my Friend Heidi, who had accompanied me, and we were taken on a most enchanting tour of the garden. Not before I promised Sister Consolata that she would receive a copy of the book.

Also my special thanks go to my sister-in-law Regina, the wife of my Brother Toni. She so very kindly gave me all the documentation and numerous photos she still had from her husband. When I asked her if she would give me some of Toni's photos, not only did she give me some of them, but all of them!

Also my special thanks go to Lilian Diehm, the daughter of Sepp our cousin, and his grandson Thomas Diehm. To both of them I am greatly indebted, for their never ending patience with telephone calls and for answering my numerous emails. Also for the photos Thomas sent me. Thank you.

A very special thank you goes to my niece Christl. She turned out to be a real treasure. Every question I sent to her in an email, she answered by return.

My thanks also go to my distant cousin Leni Gutjahr, who gave me permission to write about her experiences after WW2.

Also my thanks go to Irmgard Wäsler (now Hubauer) the niece of Benedikt Off who saved my bother Shorsh's life 60 km from Moscow. She so kindly got in touch with Beni's daughter-in-law to ask for a photo which I wanted to include in my book. After only 5 days I had three photos delivered by post.

My very special thanks go to all the people who supplied me with information about the deportees from the Sudetenland.
A very special thank you goes to my friend Hanne.

Also a very special thank you goes to my friend Margaret Barker, a published writer herself, who gave me encouragement I sorely needed. She gave it with kindness and professional knowledge, when I gave her some chapters from this book to read. Here are her words: "Lisa, you must write this book, it is very important that you do!" I shall always be grateful to her for those encouraging words.

Foreword

I hope very much that you the reader will find this book interesting, and perhaps somewhat informative.

I am not a historian, but I can assure you that to the best of my knowledge, all the dates and events in this book are correct. I personally researched the information about the convents and the nuns using the historical records in the archives at the Mother Convent, Unterer Anger, in Munich.

I was lucky enough to have Toni and Shorsh's Wehrpass (military service record booklets) where I could find all the dates and details of battles and military manoeuvres. As much as possible I have used the current names for places and battle sites, however in some cases I was obliged to use the German names as cited in the Wehrpass.

Concerning the deportees from the Sudetenland, the accounts are from personal interviews, either conducted by myself during research trips to Ismaning, or by Resi Riesinger and translated from her book, The Chronicles of Ismaning, and used with her kind permission.

As much as possible I have tried to verify all my memories with my family, friends and the people of Ismaning, who lived through all these events alongside me.

I am also not a professional writer, but I did the very best I could. I would be grateful if you could keep that in mind and not judge me too harshly if the writing is not to the highest standard, but consider the many hours of work I devoted to this book.

May we learn to live, to love, to tolerate and understand,
And then may God be pleased that he created Man.
Lisa Frei, 1998.

My Family Tree

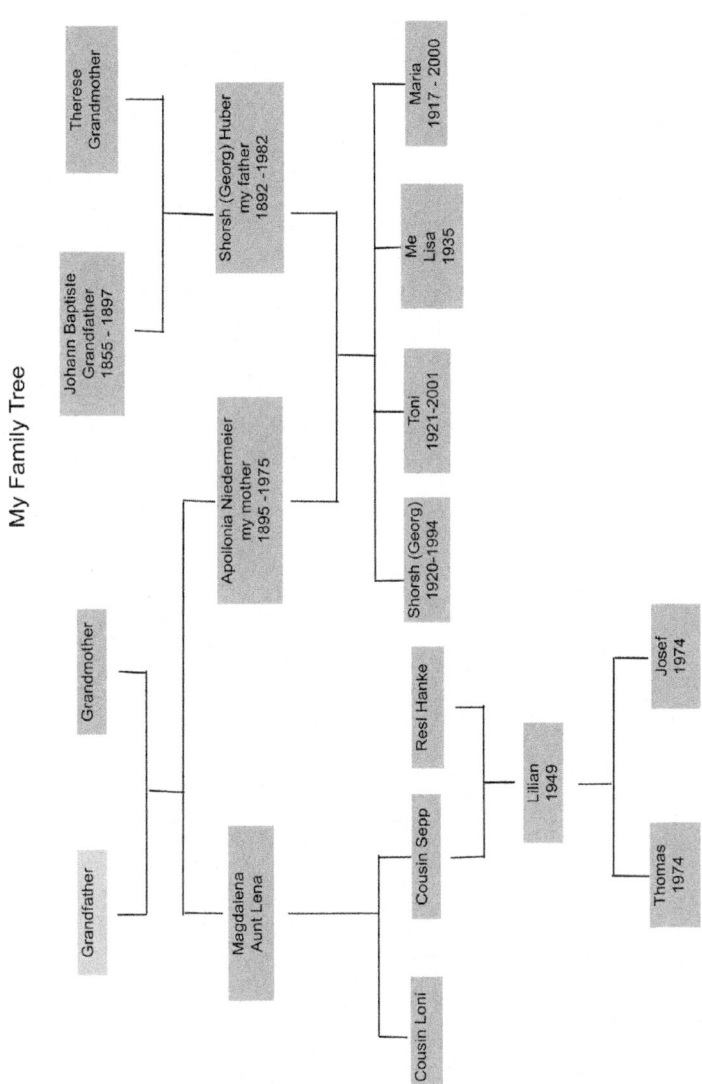

Die Strasse der Gebirgsjäger

Chapter One

A short history of the village of Ismaning.
The birth of my father and his siblings.
The tragic death of my grandfather.
School and work for father and his brother.
Christmas on the farm.
Father's late Education.

Both my parents were born in the 19th century - only just. Father, Georg Huber, was born in Ismaning on 14th April 1892. Back then it was a small farming village, 15 km to the north of Munich, the capital of Bavaria. The name Georg is Shorsh in Bavarian, the pronunciation left over from the time when Bavaria was a kingdom and it was fashionable to speak French at court.

There was not much industry in Bavaria at this time, it was mainly agriculture. People used to earn their living working on farms. My grandfather, Johann Baptist Huber, however, earned a decent living as a cobbler. My father was the youngest child of seven children. The oldest son Johann (Hans for short) was born in 1883, then came Therese (Resl for short) in 1884, after Therese came a little gap until Anna followed in 1887, then came Katharina (Katy) in 1889, with the two youngest boys to follow; Anton (Toni) in 1890 and the last one, my father, Shorsh, in 1892.

The inhabitants of Ismaning counted approximately 2000, which in the late 19th century was classed as a large village. It comprised of a church, a school, a convent and several Wirtschaft (pubs) and small shops. The community was quite self sufficient. The village brook, the Seebach, still now, as then, meanders right through the village. It starts at a small lake called the Eisweiher, at the south of the village and flows past the church and the old school, the vicarage and towards The Mill, an old restaurant, still owned by the same family, now the third generation. The brook then travels on through the park called Hain with its gym hall, then north to the outskirts of the village, veering north-west, joining the river Isar, the green Isar. This river really does flow green. Somebody once said to me that it was the forest which flanks the river that makes the water look green. It starts its journey

1

in the Wendelstein Gebirge, in the Alps. From there it travels to the north, to Munich and on to Ismaning and further north to Freising, a well known bishopric in Bavaria. Once it leaves Freising its next destination is Passau where it ends its long journey and joins the Danube.

The Eisweiher, in Ismaning is still to this day, as it always was, used in the winter for the very serious business of Eisstockschiessen (curling as it is called in English). The Eisweiher is ideal for this sport as there is hardly any movement in the water and consequently the ice is very thick come December and January. Weekends and holidays, the Eisweiher can be quite crowded as young and old enjoy the frozen lake. That small lake provides joy and amusement throughout the year, with an extensive pine forest surrounding it, making it a spot of beauty. But it had its uses in other ways. In years gone by, before refrigerators came on the scene, Wirtschaft owners used to cut blocks of ice from the lake to fill their ice boxes in their cellars, to keep the beer cool or anything else that had to be kept cool. Those ice boxes were literally just big wooden boxes.

The brook, too, had its uses. Washing of course was done by hand, no washing machines! After housewives had finished the hard work of getting the clothes clean, they would put all the wrung washing into big tin baths and on small carts pull them to the brook. There, small stiles over the water were provided for the women to kneel on and rinse the laundry in the fresh water of the brook, thus saving water and consequently money. Fresh water from the brook was free, whereas tap water had to be paid for.

On the east, the village was flanked by large fields of wheat and rye and most especially by large cabbage fields. Beyond those fields we could see the Alps in the distance on a clear day. People would say: We can see the mountains, it will be raining soon. They were always right.

The soil around the village is well suited for growing cabbage, and it is grown in abundance. It is white, hard, cabbage, which is shredded and used for Sauerkraut. That is precisely why the German soldiers got the nick name Krauts in the Second World War

Ismaning is well known in Bavaria and Germany for its excellent quality of cabbage. Years ago when I lived near King's Lynn, in Norfolk, I had bought a tin of Sauerkraut at a well known supermarket, and to my utter surprise it said on the tin Ismaninger Sauerkraut.

My father was born into a warm and cosy family. He never grew tired telling me how happy he was and how exciting and wonderful life was then. Now, it does not surprise me that life then seemed to him idyllic, as this happy time was so tragically cut short. How often I heard him say: "I wouldn't have wanted to be born anywhere else, or into any other family, the only thing I wish" he would say, "is that my father had lived longer." His bright blue eyes would look incredibly sad. I so well understood, as I knew how I was deprived of my grandfather.

The family lived in a very small house, not just by today's standards, it was considered very small then. I never could imagine how a family with seven children could live comfortably in a house with one room downstairs and one room upstairs. I could not believe that they could possibly be happy. He soon proved to me that I was very wrong. With great joy he explained the outlay of the house.

"Yes, the house was small. Father and Mother slept downstairs, we children slept upstairs. We had two double beds pushed on opposite sides against the walls. Mind you, the double beds consisted only of two single beds pushed together. In one double bed slept the boys and in the other the girls. We slept top to toe, which meant my brothers could feel my feet and I could feel theirs. Of course we had great fun tickling each other's feet." After all those years he still had to chuckle while telling me.

Between the beds against the wall stood a large wardrobe housing all the family's clothing. The two double beds and the wardrobe completed the furniture in the upper room.

"You see," he would continue, "there was still enough room for us children to play in when it was cold in the winter or when the weather was too inclement in the summer to play outside. And I bet you anything you wouldn't believe that we had central heating."

3

I just laughed. "Of course I don't believe it, there was no such thing as central heating in the 19th century."

He always did enjoy rousing my objections.

"Ah," he said, "If you lived in a very small house you could have central heating. You see, when mother had a fire in the oven range and left the kitchen door open, the heat rose and warmed our bedroom as well, now isn't that central heating?"

I had to agree with him, it was a kind of central heating. The house fitted snugly into the triangular corner where the road forked, to the right leading out of the village towards the east, past the cemetery, across the railway lines, to a small town called Aschheim. To the left the road would lead along fields towards farms. My father only remembered the house as a wonderful and warm home for the whole family, with lots of laughter and happiness. Father never lost that lovely contagious laughter, there was always a little smile tucked away in the corners of his bright blue eyes. It is not surprising that he had happy memories of that time, as he was only five years old when his father was killed and life changed so tragically. As I mentioned before my grandfather was a cobbler and he had a most unusual name. He was called Johann Baptist.

The little house was known as the Schuster Häusl (Cobbler's Cottage). I cannot imagine that it could have been easy for my grandmother, living in the cobbler's cottage with seven children, an outside well and her husband busy with his cobbling in the kitchen. It must have been a nightmare. But then I am used to the luxuries of the 20th century with central heating, washing machine and all.

Once when reminiscing again, father looked at me quizzically. He had guessed my thoughts and said: "I know what you are thinking, but you are wrong. Life wasn't as hard as you think for my parents. People were very undemanding then and we had enough to eat, and plenty of clothes to keep us warm in the winter. Father could even afford to go to the Wirtschaft on Saturday evenings for a pint or two of beer." Actually, a litre or two in Bavaria, a litre was called a Mass.

"He wasn't a heavy drinker and never came home drunk. Mother of course stayed at home, looking after us children."

Women did not go to the Wirtschaft in those days.

Then came the fatalistic day - 18th of June 1897 - my grandfather was just 42 years old. It was Saturday and as usual he went to his favourite Wirtschaft for a couple of pints, but already after the first pint he started complaining of stomach pains. It was then that one of the local jokers fell about laughing and between shrieks of laughter he told my grandfather that he had laced his beer with rat poison. This man came from a family of jokers who delighted in jokes of that nature. Yet never had they had such dire consequences. Grandfather went straight home, to the surprise of his wife, he had been gone barely half an hour, but when he eventually told her what had happened she went straight to fetch the local doctor who came back with her. What exactly the doctor did I have no knowledge of, as my father did not know. But he did know that the doctor pressed him hard to name the culprit. Grandfather never did name him. Of course, he did not think that he would die. Yet as the night progressed grandfather deteriorated. He suffered terrible stomach pains and his whole body was racked with pain and towards 4 o'clock on 18th of June 1897 he died, leaving a widow with seven children. The youngest, my father, was only five years old.

I know that it was because of his father's tragic death that he never allowed practical jokes in our family. He would always say: "If you are truly funny, you don't need practical jokes."

Yet the greatest irony was when his niece married a family member of the of his father's killer. I am sure his niece never knew, as father never talked about it. But I did notice whenever her children came to visit father would leave the room. He could not bear to be in the same room with any member of that family. Because my grandfather never revealed his killer's name, his death slipped into oblivion. But then it was the 19th century.

Without a husband my grandmother could not possibly keep six children. The oldest son, Hans, who was 16 years of age, had already left home and was working at a local farm where he also lived. It was quite usual that farmhands lived on the farm they worked for.

In 1897 social services did not exist, consequently neither did benefits. Therefore grandmother could not keep the six children. She found them places on farms around the village and also in adjacent villages. The two younger boys Shorsh, my father, and Toni, two years his senior, were taken by a wealthy farmer who was also a distant relation of the family, whose farm was in walking distance from the Cobbler's Cottage. Although related, the boys had to work for their living, even father at the tender age of five. It was work before school and work after school. Homework was discouraged. Studying was totally unimportant, but physical work was. Studying was not regarded as work. The attitude was that people who study have two left hands, which meant that with a pair of left hands instead of one right hand and one left hand one couldn't possibly do physical work. Therefore if a person did not do physical work it was said: "He is a left -hander." The idea was that children had to learn to work as early as possible and with no parents around that was just what they had to do. In the summer the boys had to get up at 4 o'clock in the morning to go to the fields with the other farmhands who did the heavy work and the boys had to rake and turn the hey to make sure it wouldn't rot as it was used in the winter to feed the animals. This was just the kind of work a child was expected to do. At seven o'clock everybody returned for breakfast; a quick wash with cold water from a bucket which was used by everybody, usually just hands and face. Then they all went into the kitchen for breakfast - not an elaborate affair by any means - a cup of coffee or two and bread, but they could eat as much bread as they wanted and it was good bread and they had sugar in the coffee, which the boys thought was lovely. The bread the boys broke into pieces, dropped them into the coffee and spooned them out with the coffee, and father thought this was a very good breakfast. He never ceased to amaze me. In the winter he could sleep until five o'clock in the morning.

"Sometimes they did let us sleep until 6 o'clock in the winter; it was a little easier for us boys."

After they had finished helping with feeding the animals in the stables, it was time to go to school. A quick wash of hands and face, picking up their satchels and off they went to school. Barefoot in the summer and in short leather trousers, but no underpants.

"Oh, they did chafe our inside legs sometimes, especially when it was very hot, but in the winter we had long trousers and boots to wear."

When father talked about his childhood it was so matter of fact, there was never any bitterness. He never thought life was all that bad. He had a wonderful logic: "That's how things were in those days."

That was his way of thinking and perhaps his way of surviving. The fact that the farmer was a distant relation made no difference. The boys were still just used as farm hands. They were regarded as an extra pair of hands, be it only small hands, but a pair of hands never the less. Toni, father's brother, and two years his senior, found it a little easier to get used to the working routine, but needless to say it was too hard for both boys.

In the summer, school started at half-past seven and in the winter at 8 o'clock. Because of their age difference, the boys went to different classes. Toni coped well with school, but father was just too young to cope with work and school and found it difficult to keep awake during lessons. Some of the teachers compassionately let him sleep, knowing full well that he had already been up several hours working on the farm. Yet there is always one who is missed by compassion. As it happened father fell asleep in one of his classes. Suddenly he woke up in a daze and didn't know what was going on, because that brute of a teacher bombarded him with questions, which father didn't have a hope of answering. Father's silence brought that teacher into such an uncontrollable rage that he smacked father's ear so hard that he burst his eardrum. Consequently father was deaf in his left ear for the rest of his life. On the farm people noticed that Shorsh did not hear very well, but that was all. Only much later as an adult he went to see a Doctor who told him that his eardrum was burst, and that nothing could be done. Only then father knew what had happened all those years ago.

When the boys came home from school, a hearty meal was waiting for them, mostly meat and dumplings and always potato salad. But work was never far away; after the midday meal it was working in the fields again; in the summer, helping with harvesting the grain; in the autumn, picking up potatoes after they had been raked to the surface by the harrow. By then it was evening again and all the farmhands went back to the farm on horse and cart, but this was not the end of the day. Stables had to be brushed and hay and straw taken down from the hay loft to be strewn between the animals and to feed them. There was a saying: "Animals have to be fed first as they cannot help themselves." (Lucky animals! I always thought). Only then was it time for the evening meal. By then the clock would strike 7.30 p.m., the meal consisted mainly of some thick broth and bread, and lots of it. It seemed such joy to father that he could eat as much bread as he liked.

Sometimes while eating their evening meal they started nodding off, and then the farmer's wife would say: "You two had better go to sleep." She didn't have to say it twice. It didn't take two minutes until they were fast asleep.

Washing before bed was done without, as they were in too much of a hurry to get into bed. They slipped off their trousers and went to bed in their shirts. They each had their own bed, but pyjamas were something else they did without: not that they had a lot of choice.

On Saturdays, late afternoon, the boys did not have to work in the stable; instead they tidied up the farm yard and swept it with a yard brush, so that it would look tidy for Sunday when it was usual for the farmer and his wife to have visitors. After this work was done, the two boys were allowed to have a bath. A large tin bath was filled with warm water and they each had clean water. In the summer they had their bath in the yard and in the winter in the stable where it was nice and warm, but they did have to use the same towels. This the boys did not mind, it was still a luxury to have a bath.

Sunday was a time of sheer joy for the boys. For a start they didn't have to rise as early as during the week. Half past five came the call from the farmer's wife, to work in the stable of course. When the animals were fed and watered, the cows milked, which was done by the female farmhands, it was a quick wash by everybody; hands and face, as more wasn't necessary, after all they had had a bath the night before. Then a quick change into their Sunday best before they all sat down for their usual breakfast. Coffee and bread it was, no change there. At half past eight it was time to go to the Roman Catholic Church for Sunday service. Bavaria is predominantly Roman Catholic. Once the service had ended, the two boys were never in a great hurry to get home. They well knew, all that was waiting for them was work, boring tedious work, whereas just outside the church was the great temptation of the village brook with its bridges where one could look for fishes and generally have fun splashing around. They played with little sticks they threw off the bridge and quickly ran to the opposite side, looking if the same sticks would appear from under the bridge.

When father, many years later, told me of those little escapades, he had such fun telling me. He enjoyed it all over again. The excitement he felt when he saw the little stick reappear, I felt with him. Father was a born raconteur. I never grew tired of his stories. Every story was an adventure he led me into. I forgot everything around me. I was right there with him, participating and enjoying every moment. This of course was many years later when time had had the opportunity to soften the harder side of life a little.

For now he was still a little boy with only his brother Toni to feel close to. When eventually the two boys came home from church, there was always somebody to tell them off. The farmer's wife scolded them because their trouser legs were wet, although the boys did their best and turned them up, but it didn't always work, they still got wet. The farmhands were cross, because they were late doing their jobs, although they were still there waiting for them. They really had to work hard to finish before lunch, which was at 12 o'clock. The boys always thought it was worth it, to taste a little freedom.

Sunday lunch was very special. All the farmhands received a good portion of roast meat with plenty of gravy and Knödel (Bavarian dumplings), either potato Knödel or bread Knödel with potato salad and green salad. With lunch out of the way it was back to church. It was a kind of Sunday school. They had to go, whether they liked it or not. They were sent in the same way they were sent to school - begrudgingly. It was considered such a waste of time, a time that could have been much better spent working on the farm. After Sunday school the boys had permission to visit their mother in the cobbler's cottage, but at 5 o'clock they had to be back at the farm to do their jobs.

Yet Christmas was very special to them. They liked going to church. This doesn't entirely surprise me as churches in Bavaria are magical at Christmas. Even on the farm an effort was made at Christmas. It was roast goose for the midday meal with potato dumplings and salads. Throughout the downstairs rooms, little tables were decked with Stollen and biscuits, where the boys could help themselves. "It was a real feast." Father would say with his usual enthusiasm. I found it peculiar that he only talked about food and never about toys. Although I well knew the importance of food, as in the 1940s housewives found it more and more difficult to be able to buy everything they wanted, but surely not in the 19th century on a farm. So I asked him: "Didn't you ever get any toys?"

He looked at me in total surprise. "Do you know?" he said. "That never occurred to me. No we didn't have any toys."

"Not ever?" I exclaimed.

"No, not ever." And I could see how surprised he was himself. He had never even thought of toys.

"But then," he said, "what would we have done with toys? We couldn't have played with them; there wouldn't have been any time."

With a wondering look in his eyes, he was talking more to himself than to me:

"I suppose we must have had some toys at some time, maybe when we still lived with our parents, but I honestly can't remember."

I, with my elbows on the table and my chin in my left hand said: "Well then, you probably didn't have any."

That made him laugh, and in surprise I asked him, still my chin in my left hand: "Why are you laughing?"

"At your logic," he replied still laughing. Then, of course, he had to explain to me the meaning of the word logic.

To this day it surprises me that both boys learned to read and write and do arithmetic. Father managed to get a good education as an adult, as he was a voracious reader. And his love for books he passed on to me. When I was only ten years old I was as familiar with some of the poems by Goethe and Schiller as I was with the fairy tales of the Brothers Grimm. With ease I could recite Erlkoenig and Zauberlehrling, by Goethe, as well as Die Bürgschaft and Die Glocke, by Schiller. Reading to me was one of my father's most loved pastimes, and mine.

Although their life was devoid of any luxuries, they had enough food to eat, warm clothes in the winter and a warm bed to sleep in. Father thought this was a luxury in itself. Yet the bed had no mattress, instead a sack as long and wide as the bed, stuffed with straw, covered with a blanket to lie on and a thick feather duvet as cover. He thought that was lovely and warm. I believed him.

He had a wonderful disposition and expected and always saw something exiting around the next corner. He was a romantic and naturally cheerful, which helped him a great deal, not only in his years of growing up on the farm, but also in his adult life. This was something that never left him.

The Schuster Häusl, the little house father was born in and lived with his parents and siblings until he was 5 years old. (photo 1950s)

Chapter Two

The birth of my mother and her siblings.
The early death of their mother.
The marriage of their father.
Their stepmother.
The death of their father.
Remarriage of their Stepmother.

If my father had a hard life, it was because he lost his father at a very early age and consequently had to work very hard on a farm already at the tender age of five, but he knew love and throughout his life he remembered the warmth and love in those few years in the cobbler's cottage. He cherished those years all his life.

Whereas mother's life was just plain cruel. She was born on 5th August 1895 in Erding, which was then a small town approximately 15 km to the north of Ismaning. She was christened Apollonia (Loni for short) and was only 2 years old when her mother died three days after the youngest child was born: a baby boy who was christened Michael, he was the sixth child in the family. He was adopted very quickly, but the other five children were left with their father. Mother was the youngest of five, 1 year older was Magdalena (Lena for short) then came Maria (Marie for short) then the two boys Ludwig and Georg (Shorsh).

Her father owned a quarry which he worked himself and earned a comfortable living for his family. They lived in a large, spacious house. After his wife had died he quickly married again a woman who brought a small boy into the family. Taking on five children was not her ideal of marriage, but she needed to escape from the stigma of having an illegitimate child.

The children had lost their own mother and now had to accept a stepmother. My mother was often beaten by her, yet surprisingly she didn't think this as terribly bad, as her two older sisters Lena and Mary were treated with even more cruelty. Especially Mary's treatment by her stepmother was unbelievably cruel. When Mary was 6 years old stepmother used to stand her in a tin bath and pour icy cold water over her, and that was done very frequently. Also my uncle

Ludwig told me about this. But just as aunt Lena he never talked about himself. This I find peculiar, but he did tell me how badly Shorsh was treated. As punishment he was hit with switches and every time she hit him buds would fly off. Somehow this seemed of significance to him, even as an old man.

Mother once said: "At least she didn't kill us, she could have done and nobody would have cared."

To that uncle Ludwig replied: "Well, this is true enough, but she did a good job on Mary."

Aunt Mary died of tuberculosis at the age of 28. Then in 1905 their father died suddenly. Although I don't think that it was very sudden at all, because mother remembered that he often complained of stomach pains. Yet what exactly he died of the children never knew.

Now stepmother had a free hand. The two older boys had already left home and worked for farmers. Now stepmother thought it was also time for the three girls to leave. She soon found farmers in Erding for each of the girls where they had to work and earn their living.

Mother found it extremely hard to leave her home, even though it was not a happy home. She so longed to be in those familiar surroundings, that sometimes she went to see her stepmother, who was not at all interested and made sure that little Loni didn't get too comfortable. She didn't offer her anything: not a piece of bread or anything else. Mother usually stood in the kitchen leaning against a cupboard and when stepmother left the kitchen for a moment to do something else in another room, mother quickly took a sip of black coffee from the pot that usually stood on the oven range.

Soon stepmother married again and the children lost everything - home, house, quarry and everything that went with it. With both parents dead, there was nobody to care about them or fight for them.

The farm my mother was working on was an extremely hard place for her. At ten years of age she was a farmhand, the youngest one on the farm. She had to work for a living, clothes were not included. Instead she had to make do with throwaways from other women on the farm. Throwaways which were far too large for a ten year old, so she would pin them up with safety pins, also any tear was mended in the same way. She had to look after herself completely, washing, mending and all that on top of doing her jobs. Personal hygiene had second place. She found it too difficult to wash her thick black hair that she wore in plaits. The hair on top of her head she used to stroke in to place with wet hands. It looked all right, she thought, but working in the stable with animals and straw it was unavoidable that she ended up having head lice. To cure this problem the older females just cut off her hair. This took care of the head lice.

She was permitted to go to school though, but for her school was mainly for sleeping. She had kind teachers who knew she had been up since 4 o'clock in the summer and 5 o'clock in the winter, so they just left her to sleep. How she ever learned to read and write and do simple arithmetic is absolutely amazing. Sometimes at night when she went to bed she would take a piece of bread with her, but she fell asleep before she could eat it, and found it still in bed with her when she woke up the next morning.

There was no Christmas and no birthday. Never new clothes and never new shoes, just throwaways and they were always too big. Still they were clothes and shoes. Money was never spent on her. She worked every day very hard for food and a bed to sleep in. She too, like my father, slept on a sack of straw and thought it was lovely. In her circumstances wherever she put her head down would have seemed lovely. The females on the farm were not the kindest human beings one could imagine, always ready with a slap when she was too slow at her work.

At the age of 17 Mother left this farm and went to join her sister Lena, in Notzing, a farming village not far from Erding, their birth town. It was a large farm with an inn attached to it. There she started at the age of 17 and for the first time in her life proper employment with the princely sum of 3 Mark, per year. Even in those early years 3 Mark was not a fortune for a year's hard work, but if so far, one had only worked for food, then 3 Mark was quite a luxury. She worked mainly in the kitchen, but if the necessity arose she had to help out in the stable with feeding the animals.

By now mother was very pretty. She had learned to look after herself. She wore decent clothes and her black hair she wore in a bun at her neck. Her beautiful skin emphasised her hazel eyes. She worked hard and always tried to please people around her. Not everybody liked her: an older woman who usually worked in the stable was quite obviously jealous and enjoyed slapping her. To mother that wasn't new, she was beaten all her life and never learned to defend herself. The landlady liked that hardworking girl and noticed that she grew reluctant to go into the stable and often tried to avoid it, which the landlady found strange. So she observed the goings on in the stable. One afternoon at feeding time she asked mother to come into her living room and there she handed her a long handled broom and said:

"Here you are my girl, you now go into the stable and when that woman comes towards you and tries to slap you hit her with this broom as hard as you can, and don't worry if she tries to come to me to complain about you, I shall slap her just to show her how it is to be hit and never let anybody hit you again."

Mother was encouraged, but still apprehensive and when she entered the stable, sure enough that woman made straight for her. Mother was still frightened, but before that slap had a chance to descend on her face she struck out and hit that woman as hard as she could. That of course came completely unexpected to her so that she received the full force of it, and mother reinforced it by saying: "You hit me again and I'll kill you!" From then on, mother was never hit again.

My mother (left) and her sister, my aunt Lena

Chapter Three

My parents meet in Notzing.
Father was promoted to look after the horses.
Father went to prison.
My parents started courting in earnest.
Mother starts a job in Ismaning and father proposes
marriage to her.

Notzing was also a village dependant on agriculture, as this
was the main industry in the 20th century in Bavaria. By now
father was in his 20th year and frequented the Kandler Wirt
in Notzing. This was the inn where mother was working.
Soon he noticed her and didn't waste any time to ask to take
her out. He wasn't the only one, but the only one who
succeeded. That was something he was so proud of and never
missed an opportunity telling me about it. But the Kandler
Wirt was also the favourite inn of Oswald, the farmer who
had taken in my father and his brother Toni, when they were
little boys, and as Oswald and his wife had no children of
their own, kept promising the two boys that they would
inherit the farm, that gave him a reason not to pay them
decent wages. Their pay day occurred now and then. Oswald
frequented the Kandler Wirt mostly Sundays. He was very
friendly with the landlord and landlady, but most certainly
not with the kitchen staff. When Herr Oswald came
everything had to be perfect. He had dinner in the private
rooms with the landlord and landlady and the meals had to be
cooked to perfection. The table was decked with the best
linen and silver and the kitchen staff were expected to do the
necessary bowing and scraping, which of course made him
very unpopular with them.

Sometimes when my mother had a Sunday afternoon
free she would go to Ismaning to see father. It happened very
infrequently as regular working hours hadn't been invented,
but at any rate never on a Sunday when Herr Oswald came to
visit. However infrequent, one Sunday afternoon when
mother came to Ismaning to see father, they had a nice walk
through the park, when in the far distance whom did they see
but Herr Oswald. Mother noticed him first and asked Father:
"Do you know who that is?"

But father went chicken and said: "No, I don't know him."

So mother enlightened him. "That," she said, "is He-e-err Oswald!" Emphasising in disdain the Herr (Mister).

From the age of 18, father had been promoted to look after the horses and carts, which was not as grand as it might sound, for he often had to start at 2 o'clock in the morning, taking produce to Munich and manure from the breweries back to the farm. It was a three hour journey one way. The horses had made the journey so many times that they knew the way by themselves. So father just curled up on the cart and had a good sleep, which indeed did most of the farmhands from the village, but it was prohibited by law to sleep on the cart when in charge of horses. It was also prohibited by law to crack the whip, which young men liked to do and displayed considerable skill at it. Unfortunately one keen policeman caught father sleeping on the cart and immediately gave him three days in Stadlheim, a prison near Munich. Well, he thought, I already have three days in Stadlheim; I might as well enjoy myself. So he cracked the whip all the way to Munich. There wasn't much of disturbing the peace, as the road on both sides was lined with fields. He was imprisoned in a cell on his own, which he found very boring. He asked the prison guard who brought him his food: "Couldn't you give me some work to do? I am just so bored."

The guard laughed and said: "Why don't you go to sleep, you keep sleeping on the cart when you should be doing your job, now you can sleep so sleep!"

Once my parents started courting in earnest, Father saw to it that Mother was employed at an inn-farm called Angermeier, in Ismaning. She had the same job as in Notzing: kitchen-maid and helping in the stable when necessary. It was not as grand an establishment as the Kandler Wirt in Notzing, but it was familiar and the landlady worked in the kitchen herself. Mother was very happy there, perhaps Father had something to do with that. Father didn't wait long before he proposed marriage to her. They decided to wait a year until they had saved enough money to start a home. They were very happy and full of hopes for the future, but Fortuna let them down! In 1914 World War 1 started and in 1916 mother fell pregnant and father was conscripted into the German army. They were devastated. She was pregnant, had to work and when the baby would arrive she had nobody to look after it.

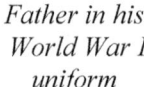

*Father in his
World War I dress
uniform*

*Father in his
World War I
uniform*

Chapter Four

Stepmother and husband come to the rescue.
14th April, a little girl is born.
Mother forgives stepmother.
Father in Belgium, at a war hospital in 1918.
Father offers his watch for civilian clothes.

Then the most peculiar circumstances followed. In desperation and after many hours of praying mother plucked up courage and visited her stepmother and husband. A husband she had never seen. To her unbelievable surprise she was most warmly welcomed. The husband was the kindest man, beside her father, she had ever met and her stepmother was a completely changed woman. As soon as mother entered the house she was offered food and coffee, which is the main beverage in Bavaria, by the woman who had never given the ten year old Loni even a piece of bread. Little Loni had had to steal a sip of black coffee when she was alone for a moment in the kitchen.

Then when mother told them that she was pregnant, without hesitation they offered to look after the baby. Mother was desperate and as they seemed so sincerely happy to look after the baby it was agreed they would look after the baby until such time when father came back from the war and they could get married.

My mother and her sister Lena both married men from Ismaning, with the surname Huber, but the two men were not related.

On 14th April 1917, a little girl was born to my mother. She called her Maria (in Bavarian Marie). As promised, her stepmother and husband took little Marie in to take care of her. Now they were even more delighted and absolutely adored her. Mother was confident that her baby would be all right, but then again, she didn't have a choice.

Mother then found every reason to forgive her stepmother all the cruelties they had to endure as children. The two people absolutely doted on little Marie, to her they were her grandparents, and to mother's relief she didn't have to have any regrets.

Father was in the army until the German capitulation in 1918. He was in a hospital for German prisoners, in Belgium. He was not heavily wounded and on the day of capitulation the soldiers heard a great tumult from outside in the street. Father went to the window and could see a multitude of people outside, running around, shouting and shots were being fired, which greatly disconcerted the soldiers. The windows and doors were locked, so father and some other patients tried to lift out the window frame, but were unsuccessful. Suddenly the door opened, an orderly appeared and with a beaming expression announced that the war was over and they all could go.

"Go where?" My father enquired.

"Well, home, where you came from." Came the answer.

Father pointing to his uniform asked: "In this?"

Quite casually the orderly said: "Oh, you'll be fine, nobody will harm you, they are too happy, we are all friends now."

But father was not convinced and made the orderly an offer. "If you bring me some civilian clothes, I'll give you my watch."

And he showed him his pocket watch. It was all that my father possessed, and the orderly couldn't resist and brought him some shabby civilian clothes and father gladly handed over his watch. He knew very well that the Belgians were just as poor as the Germans. Now as he wore civilian clothes he could start walking and walk he did. It took him six weeks to get to Ismaning. He walked during the day whenever he could as he used to stop at farms and offered to work for food and somewhere to sleep. He received food and usually slept in the stable with the animals, or in a barn. He was never permitted to enter a house; they didn't trust the Germans that much. But he always managed to get food and somewhere to sleep. In the mornings he could get a bucket of water to wash, which was quite familiar for him, he had done that many times before.

Chapter Five

Father arrives in Ismaning.
Father leaves the farm and starts work at the paper mill. With this job comes a flat.
They get married in 1919.
My two brothers are born.

When he finally arrived in Ismaning, looking like a vagabond with a six-week-old beard, he was hardly recognisable. Mother of course was overjoyed. Father left the farm when he managed to get employment at the local paper mill and with this job came a flat in a three-storey house, which was called Höglhaus, near the mill. For my parents this was just the most wonderful thing that could have happened. It was the first time in their lives they had a place of their own. The flat consisted of two rooms on the second floor, no bathroom, but cold water, a shared toilet for everybody living in the house and a wood burning stove-cooker. Saturday was bath day, which was done in a tin bath in the kitchen-cum-living room. A change of water for everyone in the family proved to be impracticable, as father had to carry the tin bath with water downstairs and pour it into the yard. Therefore a change of water for everyone was a luxury done without. The flat was well furnished with bits and pieces given to them by friends and neighbours. In 1919 they got married and then were able to take back their little daughter. It was hard for her grandparents to give her up. Once her grandfather walked all the way from Erding to Ismaning to see her, 15 km. Mother understood how hard it must have been for them, as she herself had had to part with Marie when she was only a baby. So she made sure that they could have her as often as possible and indeed, once Marie went to school she spent every school holiday with her grandparents (To her they were her real grandparents).

On 2nd April 1920, my brother Georg (Shorsh) was born and the flat became a little crowded, especially when on 15th December 1921 my brother Anton (Toni) was born, but my parents were happy. It was no hardship for them to save hard. Their dream was to buy a plot of land and build a house of their own.

Chapter Six

The house, An der Isarau 13 - back to saving again.
At two years of age Toni is found floating in the brook.
The landlord threatens my mother with the bailiffs.
Marie throws the fish away.
A special friendship between two women.

My mother still had a dream of building a house. She used to say: "We are going to build a house, no matter what it costs!"

With sheer determination they managed to save enough money to buy a decent size plot from the local council on the Isarau, on the Westside of the village, near the forest and two minutes walk from the Isar. The address was An der Isarau 13, it was back to saving again. In the meantime they were still living in the Höglhaus and just across the road was the Seebach, the brook that meandered right through Ismaning, gently made its way towards the River Isar.

One fine summer's day in 1923, mother was busy doing her washing and the two boys were playing in the yard - so she thought - but somehow they managed to get across the road and were playing by the brook. They enjoyed splashing around with water. Somehow Toni must have slipped and fell in. Fortunately another tenant from the Höglhaus happened to come along the road and saw something floating in the brook. She only saw Toni's blond hair and at first she thought it was a piglet, when she saw Shorsh running along the brook calling: "Toni come out! Toni come out!"

Now Anni Finkenzeller, that was the lady's name, realised that it was no piglet swimming down the brook, but Toni. Dressed but still in her slippers, she jumped into the brook and rescued Toni. Of course Anni lost her slippers. Shorsh always remembered how peculiar it looked when the slippers, neatly side by side, floated down the brook.

Now my parents were even more determined to move to An der Isarau 13, with houses on one side and fields on the other. How much safer it would be for their children. Although they saved every penny they could, they still had to pay the rent for their flat, which meant they had to go on waiting before it was possible to receive a mortgage from the bank. Paying the rent was an additional burden; therefore the rent was not always paid on time, which on one day brought the landlord to visit. It was not a particularly favourable day, mother felt harassed and when the landlord appeared asking why they hadn't paid the rent, saying that if they stayed behind with their payments, he would have to send the bailiffs.

Mother snapped: "And what exactly do you want to take from us? Look around." And with that she picked up Toni asking: "Do you want him or one of the other two? As you can see, I haven't got anything else."

The landlord, who was also the owner of the paper mill and knew both my parents, turned and left. On the way down the stairs he met Anni Finkenzeller, who had rescued Toni from the brook some days earlier, and said to her:

"I just saw Frau Huber, it is impossible to talk to that lady? She just offered me her son as payment for the rent." Shaking his head he left.

Of course Anni thought this was hilarious and so did everybody else in the house. The landlord never came back and my parents always managed to pay the rent, not always exactly on time, but they always paid.

Mother found it terribly hard to live with three children in a two room flat. Father was an optimist and kept saying: "We'll manage, you'll see, we'll have our house one day. We just have to wait a little longer."

Father was not blind to hardship, but he was always optimistic, he could see what they had achieved and knew they would achieve more. Mother understandably found it hard to wait and save enough for the bank to let them have a mortgage so that they could start building their house, which meant that sometimes it was difficult for her to control her irritability, no more so as when she asked my sister Marie to go and get some fish at the grocer's-cum-fishmonger.

My sister was very much afraid of dogs and of spiders. If she saw either, she screamed. So when mother asked her to get some fish, at once she asked: "What shall I do if I see a dog?"

"Then throw the plate away." Came Mother's irritated answer. But naturally she didn't mean it literally, so when Marie came back mother expected to receive the fish, but there was none. After mother's astonished question, "Where is the fish?"

Marie quite innocently answered: "I saw a dog."

"And you threw the plate away!" Mother continued herself.

She was too exhausted to be cross. After all, she had told Marie to throw the plate away. She went to look for the plate as she couldn't afford to lose it and she found it, but the fish had gone, the dog had probably had it. What was worse, she had to buy some more fish. Marie was afraid of dogs and spiders all her life. My parents never did find out why.

Whenever mother could manage, she would help a farmer who was called locally Fisherbauer, although their name was Luperger, and Bauer is the word for farmer. The farmer's wife and my mother had a very special friendship. They both had a son born exactly at the same time, with only two minutes difference. My brother Shorsh and Johann (Hans) Luperger both were born on 2nd April 1920. The two women stayed friends all their lives and so did the two boys. Mother always helped out in summer and autumn at harvesting time. In the summer it was grain and in the autumn it was cabbage. The farmers had formed a co-operative and had built a Sauerkraut factory on the main road to Munich, to which they could sell their cabbage. It became a very successful and flourishing enterprise. Years later, an industrialist from Munich had another Sauerkraut factory built on the outskirts of Ismaning.

After what seemed like an eternity, came the time when my parents were granted a mortgage and could start building their house. They managed to pay the architect, but the work they had to do themselves. Father started to dig the cellar, which had to be done by hand, the same as everything else. Pickaxe and shovel, those were the only tools. Evenings and Sundays he used to work on his house. Once the cellar was dug mother was "conscripted" to be the labourer. Father made the framework and mother had to mix the concrete with a long-handled tool, at the time this was the usual tool used to mix concrete manually. There is just one drawback, the mixture is very heavy and it is absolutely back-breaking work. My parents were the first people to buy a plot, but soon all along the road the plots had been sold to people exactly in the same position as my parents, then the men helped each other out. The house had almost been finished, when my parents failed to save the money for the next instalment for the bank. It meant their house was going to be auctioned. But mother's sister Lena and brother-in-law Josef lent them the 400 Marks that they owed the bank. On the very day of the auction Mother went into the bank and gave the 400 Marks to the Manager, who said:

"I don't know how you did it? If you have stolen it, don't tell me, because I am accepting it anyway."

Mother laughed and assured him that neither she nor her husband had stolen it. To everybody's relief they could keep their house and on 29th December 1924 they moved in. The house was ready of a sort. It had no floorboards, just plain concrete, no electricity, just oil lamps, but it was their home. Nobody was happier than the children. The boys and father did the Schuhplattler with father playing the mouth organ. This is a Bavarian folk dance that involves a lot of jumping and slapping the thighs and the soles of one's shoes. It is a dance mainly for men. Very noisy! The boys thought it was absolutely delightful and nobody told them to be quiet. No wonder mother felt so harassed before. It must have been tearing at her nerves to keep three lively children quiet because of the neighbours. They knew eventually they would be able to afford electricity and floorboards. It took them only one year and they managed to pay back the money they borrowed from mother's sister and another year to save for the floorboards. Electricity was of secondary importance, as the oil lamps proved to be very efficient. It was the first time my parents could confidently look to the future.

Chapter Seven

School for the children. The kindergarten. Our convent.
Women's work in the brick factory.

The children went to the village school. Boys and girls went to separate buildings. The girls went to the convent school. Just opposite the convent, and opposite the girl's school was the school exclusively for boys, who were taught by secular teachers, whereas the girl's teachers were nuns. The Kindergarten occupied the ground floor, including the kitchen and toilets. The living quarters of the eight nuns took the entire first floor. The nuns belonged to the order of Die armen Schulschwestern (The Poor School Sisters). Those sisters played a great role in village life.

And this is how it was supposed to stay. The convent was built right in the middle of the village, with the church next to it. Six nuns used to teach, one nun, Sister Festa, was the kindergarten sister, and one nun used to do the cooking. Those ladies had their work cut out, as practically all the village children went to the kindergarten, until they started school at the age of six years. Then children started already at the age of two years. The children had their midday meal at the convent, and the younger ones still had a sleep in the afternoon. Kindergarten finished at 5 o'clock in the afternoon.

Father still worked in the paper mill and mother managed to get a job at the local brick factory, approximately 3 km outside the village. Many women worked there making bricks, men did the work too heavy for women. Actually all work there was too heavy for women, and their wages were far below the wages of men. Yet women still called themselves fortunate to have a job, as mortgages had to be paid and children had to be clothed and fed. As long as they could do that nobody complained. The women worked together and as they all found themselves in the same position they convinced each other that life could be considerably harder. Thus, they worked and even found reasons to laugh together.

As transport they used old, often rusty bicycles. One day on their way home, very busily talking usually three abreast, they completely missed seeing a huge hey cart, which they were in the process of catching up to. When they actually saw it they were almost upon it. The two women to the right and left managed to veer off and miss the hey cart, but the one in the middle, Anni Hegl, had no choice but to cycle, amongst shrieks of laughter, right into the hey cart. That brought the farmer in charge of the cart very quickly and very alarmed to the back, only to find all the women laughing and one sitting on the ground next to her bicycle, laughing as well. The farmer too, joined in the laughter. After many years, when mother used to talk about this, she couldn't help laughing.

But alas, merriment and laughter proved rare companions for those women; instead weariness and exhaustion so often joined their journey. Once at home the cooking was waiting, which was a very simple affair. Usually half a pound of beef boiled with leek or cabbage and Knödel. Pudding wasn't something known in Bavaria, not for a long time. Perhaps a cup of coffee, of which there was always a pot on the cooker. It was not always made with real coffee beans, but very often with roasted rye, a beverage drunk very much in those days.

Although tired and poor, my parents felt life was better than ever before. They managed to hold on to their comfortable house and it proved not to be too hard to pay the mortgage, as they both had jobs.

When you entered the property from the road you met four concrete steps leading up to the green wooden front door with four small windows at the top. On entering you found yourself in a narrow hall with a brown door to the right leading into the kitchen-cum-living room. There on the left stood a black oven range, which housed a water container with a copper lid, which provided the family with hot water whenever needed. On the right, against the oven range stood a small shelf to house the shoes with a curtain to hide them. This shelf was particularly useful as the shoes and socks were kept warm and dry especially in the winter. Children always come in with wet shoes and socks after playing in the snow.

Next to this special shelf, a brown wooden door led to the master bedroom, and next to it stood a Volksempfänger (radio) on a small table and in front of that was a large couch, well, it wasn't really a couch, but a mattress on four wooden legs, which father had fitted. Mother covered it with a blanket and decorated it with cushions, which made a perfectly acceptable couch. In the right corner stood a corner bench painted with poppies and wheatears and in front of that an oblong wooden table with wooden chairs on two sides. This corner bench is still to this day in the house. Next to it was a green dresser, just next to the kitchen door. Outside in the hall was a cold water tap, no hot water. Then at the end of the hall was the boys bedroom, and on the left you would find the door leading down into the cellar. Just inside the entrance door a staircase lead to the upper floor rooms. My sister slept in one of them, but the house had no bathroom. None of the houses had, but father had built a one-room outhouse where the weekly washing and bathing was done. This outhouse housed a large copper, which was heated by a fire from underneath and provided hot water and warmth when bathing. The rest of the property was a substantial yard and garden.

Chapter Eight

The great depression.
Father is made redundant. Mother's wages pay the mortgage, only just.
Father tries to sell produce.
Father gets a job. He is made redundant again.
Father starts begging.
Father has a brilliant idea - a pub is needed.

Although life was hard, people saw a result from their work and generally thought it could only turn for the better, as long as they could manage to pay their mortgage life couldn't be bad. How wrong they were! They had no idea what a short step it can be from having little to having nothing at all. Both my parents had been there before and didn't want to go there again. But 1926 came running with giant steps. Father was made redundant! He was not alone, many men lost their jobs and some even their house. Father started growing leek and other produce and sold it to a market stall holder in Munich. It went quite well at first, until most of the men in the village had the same idea. The stall holders became overwhelmed and the prices went so low that even with the best will it became a lost cause. It looked very black for the people. Mother's wage was just enough to pay the mortgage, but only just, it certainly wasn't enough to buy food as well. The farmers in the village had more men to help than they needed. Mother still managed to help some farming friends and received food in payment. Yet, however hard my parents tried it was very hard to get enough food on the table. Then father was fortunate enough to get a job at a hydraulic engineering firm called Moll, who started to build a bridge across the river Isar, 5 km upstream. He did piece work in the clay pit. The ground in Ismaning is mainly clay and as everything had to be done by hand, the men from the village dug the foundations for the engineers. Father had made himself a bicycle from oddments neighbours and friends gave him, which provided valuable transport for him, otherwise it would have been a long daily walk. The bridge is called Moll Brücke and is still in use to this day. The bicycle that he painted yellow was still going strong when I was a little girl.

Alas, eventually this job came to an end, which meant father was made redundant yet again. He knew that there was very little chance of him getting another job. Mother's job barely paid the mortgage. Father got odd jobs helping with the harvesting, but even the farmers had more help than they really needed. Mother's friend, the farmer's wife, helped as much as she could. In the end it became so difficult to put enough food on the table that father decided to go begging.

He didn't want to beg in Ismaning where he would be recognised, but he thought it would be alright in Garching, a village just across the river Isar where nobody knew him. He took a rucksack with him and off he went on his trusted yellow bicycle. He knew that begging was against the law, so he offered to work for bread because he knew very well that no farmer would pay him with money, they too had a pretty rough time keeping going. Very often a farmer's wife would ask him to cut some wood or tidy up the yard, mend a cart or a bench and he would be paid with bread or if lucky with a little smoked meat or even a few eggs. When he came home in the evenings his rucksack was usually full of food and the family had an absolute feast.

Many years later I asked him whether he had found it hard to beg, of course then I didn't know yet that only a few years hence I would do exactly the same in Ismaning. But more of that later!

For now my life was still very cosy. I crept close to him and asked what exactly he did say when he entered a farm.

"In the beginning it was hard." He said. "I felt about two centimetres high when I entered my first farm, especially when I said: Frau my children are hungry, could you give me a piece of bread? I'll do any kind of work you might have and you can pay me with bread."

He was successful, mended two wooden benches and received half a loaf of bread for it. He thought he was very lucky that he was treated kindly and with respect the first time. That gave him the courage to try another farm. If the treatment had been different at the first farm, as indeed it could have been, he didn't think it would have been so easy to continue.

"And it wasn't always hard and gloomy," he smiled as he winked at me.

"Oh, Papa, come on! Tell me about it." I begged, as I crept closer to him on the end of the bench in the living room-cum-kitchen, he puffing on his long pipe.

"Well," he said, "there was one incident which was quite humorous. You know, begging is against the law, which means you are not permitted to go into a farm and beg. Strictly speaking, I wasn't exactly begging, because I offered to work, but the police didn't accept that. So, one day I rode on my bicycle to Garching again, across the River Isar, and leant my bicycle against the wall under the kitchen window of a farm I entered. I walked into the kitchen and said: Grüss Gott (Hello) to the Bauerin (farmer's wife). She just looked at me as if to say: What do you want? I saw at once that she wasn't in a good mood, so I just asked if I could have a piece of bread, please. And without saying a word she just went to the cupboard, opened a small door, took a round loaf of bread out and with one hand she held it against her chest and with the other started to cut a piece off, and while she was cutting the bread she was looking out of the window. Suddenly she started laughing. I asked her what was funny. Still laughing she told me to look outside. And asked me what I was going to do now? I followed her eyes and saw a middle-aged, somewhat portly, policeman coming through the gate, carefully closing it behind him. I said thank you to the Frau, took the piece of bread and told her: "Watch me!"

I was out of the door, past the policeman and with one jump I cleared the gate and was down the road. I turned back and saw the policeman still standing there, so I waved to him and he shook his fist at me. But of course he didn't have a hope of catching me. Of course, I was a young man then. But listen to this; I had forgotten my trusty transportation. My bicycle was still leaning under the kitchen window. What do I do now? I thought. That policeman has surely taken it. But luck would have it that he must have forgotten it too. I think he was too angry about me getting away that he didn't think of my bicycle, because when after about an hour I crept back along the fields, not in the road - I wasn't that brave - and came nearer to the farm, past a small copse, there was my bicycle leaning against a tree. So you see we can never quite trust our first impressions. I thought the farmer's wife was in a really bad mood, and not very kind either. But she was! When I was in need of help she did just that, help me, and she didn't even know me."

Without this valuable transportation it would have been a very long walk home for him. Those stories and talks with my father are to this day my most precious memories.

Yet begging was not an occupation father treasured, to say the least, that is why one day he had a brilliant idea, so he thought! No Wirtschaft (public house) existed in the immediate vicinity. The nearest Wirtschaft was situated at the main road leading to Munich. When he told mother of his brilliant idea to open one, she was horrified.

"And where on earth would you have people sit?" Which meant - Where would the men be sitting? As only men frequented Wirtschaft, never women.

"They can sit here in this big room at the table. There is plenty of room for at least eight men, and with all the men working on their houses we will make good business."

That was when mother became very sarcastic.

"Well, of course when there is beer involved, naturally there is plenty of room for the whole street."

Mother was not pleased at Father's brilliant idea, but when he said: "It beats begging believe you me!" She became very quiet. In the heat of the moment she had forgotten her husband's daily ride on his bicycle across the Isar and she understood that her husband was desperately trying to find something else to do to earn some money. Now Mother realised that she didn't really have an argument against it. So a Wirtschaft it was going to be.

A brewery from Munich agreed to deliver beer in bottles and that was all that was needed then. Men came every evening either to take beer home or to stay a while to drink a few bottles, some of them stayed to play cards, often well into the night. It was a noisy business and Mother hated it, but now they had enough money to buy food and with Mother's wages they could pay the mortgage. It was not an ideal situation, but father felt he had to make a choice; it was either continue begging or the Wirtschaft. Understandably the Wirtschaft won.

In 1929, it just happened that a young couple were building a house next to my parent's house and had been looking for a place to live, and asked my father whether he could help out. Luckily there was one spare room in my family's house which father offered them. Very happily they accepted. It was ideal for them to live next to their plot, they could work there whenever they had some time to spare and above all the rent was very cheap. However cheap it was, it helped my parents. After one year, the couple's house had been finished, of a sort, no floorboards and no electricity, but just like my parent's they too were happy to move in.

When they moved out, the village postman, Sebastian Widmann, asked my parents if he could rent the spare room for a short while. They gladly agreed and became good friends with Sebastian. After half a year he got married and moved out.

Chapter Nine

My sister, Marie, leaves school and goes to work on the farm.
Marie comes home.
New tenants, Ludwig and Resi Zott.
1933, my older brother, Shorsh, tries to join Hitler's Youth.
Father explains the difference between the German National
Party and the Communist Party.

In 1931, my sister left school. She was 14 years old and went
into service on a farm in Fürholzen, about 25 km to the west
of Ismaning. She had no chance of finding a job of any kind
in Ismaning and in spite of Mother and Father keeping the so-
called Wirtschaft, there just wasn't enough food to feed her
as well as the rest of the family. So when my parents took her
to the farm and had to leave her there they were heartbroken.
My mother cried all the way home.

When after a fortnight they went to visit her, they found
a very miserable girl. When the farmer came into the kitchen
from working in the fields, he washed his hands in the water
container next to the cooker and put some beef into a pot. The
farmer's wife then used the very water her husband had just
washed his hands in, to boil the beef! My parents were
horrified and didn't waste a minute in taking Marie back
home.

She wasn't at home very long when the owner of the
local dairy, called Kraus, was looking for a young girl as
general help, and to everybody's delight Marie got the job.
Every payday evening Marie would buy a large loaf of bread
on the way home. Then, through well to do friends of her
boss, she got the wonderful opportunity to train, with several
other girls, as a waitress in a large hotel in Wiesbaden. The
only drawback was that she had to leave her family again.
Marie was excited, mother was dismayed and father thought
it was a wonderful opportunity.

Now there were two rooms available in the house, to
rent out. Soon again a young couple asked to rent the two
rooms. My parents became very good friends with Ludwig
and Resi Zott, the young couple who moved into the two
spare rooms. Toni and Shorsh, my two brothers, became very
fond of Ludwig. Ludwig had that rare commodity - time! He

was always up to some tricks with the boys. Mother used to bake doughnuts on Saturday afternoons. They were meant strictly for Sundays. On one of those Saturday afternoons, to cool the doughnuts, she had put them in a bowl on the windowsill in the master bedroom with the window open, as she usually did. But then, when she came to turn them she noticed some missing. This is very odd, she thought. It had never happened before and she was convinced it must have been a large bird that had feasted on her doughnuts. So she waited for the bird to return to shoo it off. To her amazement it wasn't a bird at all. Around the corner of the house, out of sight was Ludwig with the boys and with a homemade fishing rod angling the doughnuts. Mother made sure to close the window on Saturday afternoons from then on.

The money my parents received for the rent from Ludwig and Resi made a real difference to the family's life. There was political unrest, but so far it hadn't affected their way of life. Father wasn't interested in politics, but he was very interested in looking after his family and so far had done a very good job under sometimes very difficult circumstances.

Already in the late 1920s a movement for young boys had started called Jung Volk, which later became Hitler's Youth. The German National Party was a very up-and-coming party. Hitler's Youth was only for boys, for girls it started later and was called Bund Deutscher Mädchen known as the B.D.M. (Bond of German Girls). Father didn't think too much of the National Party. But so far they had left him alone and he left them alone.

In 1933 young boys still needed the signature of their fathers if they wanted to join Hitler's Youth. Young boys as well as teenagers flocked to join them, which was hardly surprising as each of them received a pair of brand new black boots, a brown shirt and a jacket. Shorsh, my older brother, desperately wanted a new pair of boots. He had never had a new pair of boots in his life. One day he came to father with the application form to join Hitler's Youth and asked for his signature. With a heavy heart father tried to explain to Shorsh why he could not possibly give him permission to join.

"Look," he said, "I am not a clever man, but what I can see of this party is not really to my liking. They push us around too much and I do hope people will come to their senses. This party is too radical."

But Shorsh could only think of those lovely shiny, black boots which he so dearly wanted. Father tried very hard to make him understand when he said:

"There is something fundamentally wrong with this party if they have to bribe young boys to join."

Whatever father said, Shorsh just could not understand why he should not have a new pair of boots as so many other boys. That's why he forged father's signature, and he was proud of it because he thought he did a really good job. Equipped with his form he went to the next meeting of the Hitler's Youth and was greeted by the leader with a loud: Heil Hitler! Equally loudly Shorsh answered with an enthusiastic: Heil Hitler! And handed the signed form over. To his surprise, the leader handed the form back to him and said:

"We don't want you; your father is a communist. Go home!"

Shorsh was 13 years old and had no idea what a communist was. He was angry and embarrassed and on the way home he tore the form to shreds and threw it into the Seebach, the village brook, wishing it was the Hitler's Youth leader that he was throwing in. At home he asked father, if he was a communist. At that father had to laugh and still laughing he said:

"No, of course not, I am not a communist and not a Nazi. Whatever makes you ask that?"

Then Shorsh had to tell him what he had done and thought father would be really angry with him, yet father was not angry, he knew why Shorsh wanted to join and that made his heart ache because he just did not have the money for a new pair of boots for his son. But he was angry with the youth leader. He gave a 13 year old boy the form to fill in only to reject him when he brought it back. It was doubly hard to bear for father, not only did his son not get any new boots because of him, but also because of him his son was humiliated. They well knew that Father was not a communist, but because he refused to join the Party that was good enough to brand him a communist. Father tried very hard to explain to Shorsh about the National Party.

"You see Shorsh, this was a nasty trick he played on you. He knows I am not a communist, but he enjoyed humiliating you, and through you he could get at me. This is the behaviour of thugs. You see now, I have very good reasons for not joining this party. But I don't like the communist party either; I really can't see a lot of difference between them. They are one as bad as the other. People will come to realise that both parties are too radical, and don't care for the workingman. I am not the only one who wants nothing to do with them. All those promises they make to give us food and work, how could they possibly do that?"

But the German National Party did win to form a Government.

So far things did not seem too bad, in spite of Father being branded a communist. In 1934, Shorsh now 14 years old reached school-leaving age, after eight years of Volksschule (compulsory schooling for all children). Shorsh had set his heart on becoming a carpenter, but it proved too difficult to find a place for training, therefore he accepted a farmhand's job in Oberding, about 15 km north of Ismaning. Shorsh had a bicycle that he used to come home whenever he could. When he left for the first time mother stood in the road until she could not see him anymore, crying bitterly. Then Toni said: "I am never leaving home even if my meals are only bread and coffee."

But fate did not listen. He didn't know then, that the time would come when he would be further and longer away from home than anyone else in the family.

Shorsh worked for a farmer with the surname Schreiber, in Oberding, a village to the north of Ismaning. The farmer and his wife made him very welcome and made sure he was happy working on their farm. Although he liked working there, he never stopped looking for a place as an apprentice to become a carpenter. While working there a very funny incident happened that Shorsh told me about. It was the time when people started buying radios. Shorsh's boss bought one and a neighbouring farmer as well. Soon afterwards the grandmother of the neighbouring farmer came, for some reason, to visit. Shorsh was just working in the yard, the weather was rather dull. He said to the lady entering the yard through the gate: "Tomorrow we will have very good weather; I just heard it on the radio."

The answer he received rather surprised Shorsh, as she said: "Don't lie! Our radio said that."

With that she walked into the kitchen and Shorsh stood there laughing. She quite obviously thought that the radio would say something different in every house. It was after one year of working on the farm he found a place in Markt Schwaben, a village near Oberding, to train as a carpenter. He earned two Reichsmark per week with board and lodging. He felt very lucky that he earned anything at all, as often apprenticeships did not pay anything.

*From left to right, my cousin Loni,
me at 8 years old, Tusnelda in her
B.D.M. jacket*

Chapter Ten

A young man, Franz Mösl, moves into the family house.
Franz dances a Bavarian dance, with dire consequences.
A bombshell hits the family.
Toni makes friends with a professional soldier.
My first memory.

Soon after Shorsh had left home in 1934 a young man, Franz Mösl, asked my parents if he could rent the two rooms upstairs. My parents were only too pleased and Franz moved in. He was a young man of 25 years and worked in Munich as a labourer at the SS Kaserne (SS Military Barracks). All barracks were named after Nazis.

It was the time before insurance existed, therefore all workers put a little of their wages into a kitty to be able to still draw wages should the weather be too wet for work. One afternoon it was just such an afternoon. All the workmen went into a pub nearby, to wait for the rain to stop and have a beer. One man started playing the accordion. Franz had been from a young age a member of the Trachten Verein, the folk group in Ismaning, and was a very good dancer. He got up and started to dance, doing the Schuhplattler, slapping his thighs and hitting the soles of his shoes with his hands. In a corner away from the workmen, two Nazis in uniform with rifles were sitting - they always had their rifles with them. The workmen took no notice of the two men in uniform, as they were busy enjoying themselves. Suddenly while Franz was dancing the two got up and hit him to the floor with their rifle butts and as an excuse they accused him of making the communist salute, because while slapping his thighs and the soles of his shoes Franz lifted his arms in the air as part of the dance. The communist salute is lifting one arm while making a fist. Franz did nothing of the sort, he was just dancing. They dragged him outside, bundled him into a car and drove him to Tuerken Strasse, in Munich. That's where the Nazis had a torture chamber in the cellar. There they beat him within an inch of his life. They kept him there for two days. My parents wondered why he did not come home, he had never done that before, they hoped it was a girlfriend who was keeping him away from home. Yet, they still worried about him, they had heard about too many dreadful incidents that were going on. On the third day in the middle of the night, mother heard him coming in and noticed the peculiar way he walked up the stairs. She woke father and they went upstairs and found Franz lying on the landing floor covered in blood. When they took off his jacket, mother found blood in his jacket pockets. They put him on his bed, washed him and did not find one spot on his body that was not bruised.

Franz survived! For three weeks he could not go to work, yet nobody came to inquire and when he went back to work nobody asked him where he had been. He did not go to the police or any other authority to complain about his treatment, this would not have been very wise, as he well knew it would have been too dangerous for him and it might well have been that he would have forfeited his life.

Then a bombshell hit my parents. I was the bombshell. My mother at 39 years-of-age and father 43 years old, already having three children almost grown up, were not exactly over the moon. Mother had to give up her job, which meant only one income. Things for a while were tight again, but now there was only Toni at home. Shorsh was still working on the farm in Oberding and came to visit every Sunday afternoon on his bicycle when he was free until 5 o'clock, when he had to be back to help in the stable. It was an hour's ride home and back which gave him about two hours at home. The two boys, Shorsh and Toni, wanted a little sister and as the time of my birth came nearer, Shorsh came very frequently. But then came Christmas and the snow and Shorsh came home less often. The farmer, who knew how desperately my parents wanted to see him, at some point told him: "I have heard from your mother, you have a little sister."

From then on, whatever the weather, Shorsh would ride home. But for Christmas that year he could not ride home as the snow was too deep. I was born on 10th January 1935. That year father sold the Wirtschaft to a friend, Hans Blum, who lived on Am Isarberg road, a road running parallel to An der Isarau, where my parents lived. In spring 1935 father and a friend from the village, who was very much of the same mind as my father concerning the National Party, were offered a job in Neustadt on the Danube, working to build the autobahn. They only came home weekends. If you were offered a job in 1935 you did not decline, you accepted with a smile, especially my father and his friend as both men had a somewhat dubious reputation as neither of them had joined the National Party. Father used to call his friend Schwegler, this was his surname and indeed he was known throughout the village as Schwegler. I never did find out his forename.

In 1937 Toni, at 16 years-of-age, made friends with a professional soldier, Off Beni, who lived in our road. Off was his surname and Beni his christian name. It is an idiosyncrasy of the Bavarians to say the surname before the christian name. That young soldier was always called Off Beni by everyone in the road. Toni found him fascinating. He thought the uniform was great! And the rifle. Then one day Off Beni gave him a Flobert (a small calibre rifle) with some ammunition and taught him to shoot. Toni was over the moon, but as they say: Boys will be boys. With Toni it was: Toni will be Toni. For him shooting was not quite enough. He wanted to make more noise than the Flobert would make. So, the ammunition was not quite enough for him, therefore, he stuffed the barrel full of newspaper and rammed it down with a stick, thinking it would make an enormous bang, and it did! He pulled the trigger and there was an almighty bang and the Flobert was gone, it had exploded, Toni had nothing in his hands. Mother rushed into the garden to find Toni ashen faced. She did not know whether she should be angry or glad that he was still alive. The whole neighbourhood came looking to see what had happened. Toni was just incredibly lucky to still be alive. All he had tiny little splinters in his arms and fingers. The following spring, when father was digging the garden, he found the barrel of the Flobert - that was all. Needless to say Off Beni never gave anything else to Toni again. He said to father: "That boy is dangerous! I taught him to shoot and he was good, but he is unbelievable."

Off Beni, several years later in the Second World War saved the life of my older brother Shorsh. But more of that later.

Christmas Eve 1935, sixteen days before my first birthday, Christmas celebrations were well on the way, as is usual in Bavaria. Christmas Eve is the most important day at Christmas, it is a day strictly for family. The Christmas tree is lit and presents are shared, but Christmas dinner is on Christmas Day. On this particular Christmas Eve, I was standing by the settee, holding on for support, as babies do when starting to walk. Toni kneeling on one knee in front of me with his arms stretched out, was encouraging me to let go of the settee and walk towards him. He did that for a while with me looking intensely at him and the family looking on. Then suddenly I let go of the settee and ran into Toni's arms, flinging my arms around his neck. All the family absolutely roared and I still remember this. From that day on I was walking.

Toni had left school that year, being 14 years of age, then the school-leaving age in Bavaria. He was training to be a joiner in Munich at the firm of one of our cousin's. He stayed there one year, but left when his friends started training as bricklayers and earned more than he did. Our cousin, who was also called Toni, Toni Haberl, was very dismayed about that and so was our father because Toni Haberl was his sister's son. But father understood that his son wanted to be with his friends. In 1936 Toni started his three year apprenticeship as a bricklayer with a firm called Habereder a well known builder in Unterfföhring, a village 5 km south of Ismaning, towards Munich.

Father and his friend Schwegler now worked as labourers in Munich at the barracks. It was quite ironic that those two branded as communists now worked building the Adolf Hitler Kaserne.

1936 my father in Heufeld, Germany, working on the autobahn (Father on the right, his friend Schwegler on the left)

Chapter Eleven

Shorsh gets his boots, and trains to be a carpenter.
His master forgets to deduct the money.
Shorsh passes his exam.
Franz gets married.
My sister has a baby boy.
Emil, my sister's baby boy, develops Cradle Cap.

In 1936 Shorsh left the farm where he was working, in Oberding and started an apprenticeship to become a carpenter in Markt Schwaben only a few km from Oberding. He was delighted and so were my parents as they well knew how desperately Shorsh wanted to become a carpenter. Besides, he earned a regular wage, two Reichsmark per week in the first year and three Reichsmark in the second year, which went up to four Reichsmark in the third year. His apprenticeship came with board and lodging. The master-carpenter and his wife, Mr and Mrs Mittermeier, were the kindest couple Shorsh could have hoped for. Mr Mittermeier was a real master in his trade and beside that an excellent teacher. Shorsh called him Master and his wife Lady (in Bavarian Moaster and Moasterin). They had no children of their own and took Shorsh to their hearts. Sunday was his day off, when he could do whatever he liked - sheer delight! One evening, after the first week, his master saw that Shorsh was wearing a pair of beautiful, black, shiny boots. The master was surprised as he well knew Shorsh could not possibly afford a brand-new pair of boots. Shorsh told him with glee that he had bought them on hire-purchase, paid one Mark and would continue to pay one Mark every week until the boots were paid for. His master smiled and said: "No, don't do that." He gave him the money to pay for the boots in full saying: "Here is the money, go and pay for your boots and I'll deduct it in small amounts every week from your wages."

He did that for a few weeks, but then kept forgetting it and when Shorsh reminded him he would say: "Oh, I forgot. I'll deduct it next week."

And this went on for some time, then Shorsh stopped reminding him, but never stopped appreciating it. At last

Shorsh had his new boots and he did not need the Nazis to get them for him.

In 1939 he completed his training as a carpenter, yet he had never attended a training college. His master did not think it necessary as he could teach him everything he needed to know. After the end of his three years training, Mr Mittermeier entered him for the exam in a training college in Munich for his Gesellenprüfung (the exam needed to become a journeyman). On the eve of the exam, Mr. Mittermeier gave Shorsh a book to look at with the words: "Look at it, it might help you tomorrow."

The following day Shorsh went equipped with this book to Munich to sit for the exam and had quite a surprise. When he was handed the exam paper he had no idea what it said. The professional expressions were all in high German, whereas all his master had ever taught him was in the Bavarian dialect. Every professional term Shorsh had ever heard was in this dialect. So, he put a line through what was written on the front of the paper he had received, turned it over, opened the book his master had given him and on the back of his exam paper he worked out and drew the plans for a spiral staircase, an exercise he found in the front of the book. Shorsh liked it and thought this was a good exercise and set to work. He worked it out in every detail and was very pleased with himself, and also was the first in the class to hand his paper in, but was a little surprised when the examiner looked at him somewhat doubtfully, as it was a different paper to what he expected. A few days afterwards, Shorsh received a letter to see a professor at the training college where he had done his exam a few days before. So, again equipped with his book he went to the training college where a professor cordially received him.

"Sit down," he said. "And tell me why you crossed out the exam paper and drew this spiral staircase on the back instead?"

Shorsh showed him the drawing in the book and explained to the professor:

"This drawing I could understand and I knew I could work it out, but those words on the front of the paper, I just couldn't understand. My master never used those words."

"Well," said the professor. "He must be some master, if he taught you that. This is an excellent piece of work and really deserves top marks, but I am really sorry that I can't give you top marks, because you didn't do the work you were asked to do, but I can give you a grade lower."

Instead of a 1, which in Germany is the equivalent to an A, Shorsh received a 2, which is the equivalent to a B in England. Then as a fully-fledged carpenter, he started to work for a large company called Heilmann & Littmann, in Munich.

In 1936, Franz Mösl, the young man who rented the two rooms upstairs in my parent's house, got married to a nice young lady called Anni. In 1937 their happiness was complete when Erich their baby boy was born, but when he died at two years-of-age from German measles they were devastated.

In 1939 on 8th August, on the very day of Anni's own birthday, their baby girl was born, whom they also called Anni. It was quite natural that we should become good friends and indeed we still are and with her brother Johann who was born in 1940. Also on 15th July 1940 my nephew Emil was born to my sister Marie. Her fiancé, already in the army, asked for the baby boy to be called Emil. This was the last Marie heard from him. It was much later that she learned he had married another lady.

As it was the time of the Third Reich, every able-bodied man or woman had to work, therefore my sister was not permitted to stay at home to look after Emil. As the father was a soldier, the state paid my mother to look after Emil to make it possible for my sister to keep working. Anni and my mother now had four children to look after and they really had their work cut out for them. The two baby boys managed to keep those two women working day and night. Emil, soon after his birth, developed Milch-Schorf (Cradle Cap) and Johann could not digest milk. So both the boys had to be nourished without milk. This Cradle Cap is a terrible affliction. In 1940 there was no treatment for it and no cure. The babies suffered terribly. Their whole face and only their face, would be covered in blisters, which itched. All the Doctors could say was that it would not leave any scars and that after nine months it would start to heal and the baby could then drink milk, and so it was. Both the boys recovered well and the four children in the house made a merry band.

On the whole life was comfortable for the two families in the house. In 1938 my parents had saved enough money for electricity to be installed and food could still be bought.

Chapter Twelve

A friend of father's joins the Party.
Hitler's Army marches into the Rhineland.
The infamous election.
Toni and his friend buy an NSU motorcycle together.
The two young men thought life was so good.

In the early 1930s Korbinian Huber, a close friend of father, who used to mend watches in his kitchen, joined the Party to the dismay of father. Father tried to talk him out of it, but Koorby, that's what father called him, was convinced that it was the best thing he could do. He still sometimes came to see father. Koorby's daughter was friendly with my brothers as they were of the same age. Koorby tried to persuade father to join the Party. Father could see nothing good in the Party and as always was very outspoken. Consequently they used to argue: Koorby for the Party and father against it. Koorby came less and less. On his last visit on his way out he said to father: "Shorsh," this was also father's name, "be careful. Don't be too generous with your opinion."

Father looked at him and knew that this was a warning, and he said to mother: "Did you see how drawn he looked? It's the Party that's doing that to him."

Now that Koorby was in the Party there was no way out. If you joined the National Party, you did not leave, that is if you wanted to continue to live. I remember Korbinian so well, as he became Bürgermeister (mayor), which he was until 1945. He was a small man and in the Nazi uniform he looked even smaller.

On 7th of March 1936, the German army which shouldn't really have existed according to the Treaty of Versailles, marched into the independent state of the Rhineland, as it was practically German anyway Hitler's army wasn't stopped. That the Rheinland was neutral didn't bother the German chancellor in the least. After all he was the mighty German chancellor. In 1938 the infamous election was held, and we all know what a farce that was. My mother told me once: "Voting was compulsory. The election place was in the girl's school. At the entrance stood a Nazi in uniform with a rifle across his shoulder. In the room was a long table and sitting behind it was another Nazi with election forms in front of him. He pointed to the box allocated for the National Party and said: 'Make your cross here.' I felt so intimidated I couldn't see the name of any other party. I am sure there wasn't another party, even if there had been, I wouldn't have dared to vote for it. I just made my cross, and went out as quickly as I could. It was so frightening."

The National Party was victorious with 99.6 % of votes. Why not 100%? That wouldn't have made the farce any greater. What a boost for the German chancellor! I still wonder; did he believe that? Also in 1938 the German army had liberated Austria. What Austria was liberated from nobody knew and nobody asked. In my family life was good. My parents had exactly what they had wished for and worked for so hard: a house of their own. Shorsh lived at home again as he worked in Munich. Toni was still training as a bricklayer and my sister Marie worked in Munich in a restaurant and came home frequently. Shorsh and Toni used a small room downstairs as their bedroom. The room was just large enough for two single beds on either side against the walls, with a narrow corridor in the middle, and a green wardrobe to the left of the door. This concluded the furniture. One day Toni announced that he with his best friend, Franz Glas, had decided to buy an NSU motorcycle together. Father agreed and so did Franz's parents. It didn't take long before they had saved enough money to buy one. Franz was also training to be a bricklayer, and together they built a small garage in the garden of Franz's parents, just big enough for a motorcycle and a couple of chairs. They had their own little den, a little retreat after work with a few bottles of beer and a motorcycle to cruise around on. Yes, life was good!

Two friends, Toni and Franz, before WW2

Chapter Thirteen

Ismaning 1939, the nuns have to leave the convent.
Famers start to get worried.
The last day for the nuns in the convent.
Mother tries to explain the Party to me and why the nuns have to leave the convent.
WAR!

Ismaning 1939 - since 1865 eight nuns had lived in the convent. Four nuns, qualified teachers, taught the girls in the schoolhouse opposite the convent, but on 16th April 1939 they had to leave. The Nazi Party did not think that nuns could possibly bring up children to be good German adults. The emphasis was of course on German, which meant pure German. Children had to be carefully taught what it meant to be a German: confident, upstanding, disciplined and only the Führer to be adored. If there was a God then it was the Führer. Nuns couldn't possibly compete with this ideology, nor did they want to. The four nuns went back to the Mother convent, named Unterer Anger, in Munich.

For one year longer, the kindergarten was run by the four nuns still in the convent, with two nuns in the kitchen and two nuns running the kindergarten. All children went to kindergarten; it was a natural thing to do. Whether a boy or girl, we went to the kindergarten. Sister Festa, the nun running the kindergarten, had been in the convent the longest. She knew everybody including our parents. Only much later I realised how hard these ladies must have worked. Most of us children were only two years of age when we started and still had to have our sleep at midday. Sister Festa was a remarkable lady, small bright eyed with a never-ending imagination. I kept in touch with her until she died in 2005, at 100 years-of-age. She was one of those ladies one is proud to have known.

On 1st April 1940 they were given notice to leave the convent with immediate effect. It was a very short, succinct and cold notice from Koorby, the Bürgermeister. Was it really from the man I knew so well?

Now the farmers started to get worried and decided to take matters into their own hands, and asked for the nuns to stay in the village. The farmers still had some power as Hitler needed them. The nuns got permission to stay. At first they were offered a small flat, by a family in the village, but it proved too small for four of them, two nuns would have had to sleep with a neighbour. Then the farmers offered them, on the second floor of the local sauerkraut factory, a suitable flat consisting of three rooms, kitchen and some storerooms. The farmers saw to it that it was renovated and electricity installed. The Mother convent was happy with this arrangement, as the nuns could still work for the church by doing needlework, but spiritual work in the Third Reich was absolutely out of the question. By doing needlework for the farmers, the nuns helped to contribute to their keep. The rent was twenty Reichsmark per month, but it was not an absolute guarantee that they could stay. The nuns had to agree, should an employee be in need of this flat, to vacate it with four week's notice, but as it turned out this never happened.

The kindergarten was, on the day the nuns left, taken over by secular nursery teachers as was the Volksschule. All teachers had to prove they were true Aryans - if there is such a race - and of course be members of the NSDAP (Nationalsozialistische Partei Deutschlands) in short Nazi Party. Choice was a luxury people had to do without. It was to be a party member or forced labour, and this didn't mean working in your profession.

On the last day before the nuns had to vacate the kindergarten, all the children received small presents. A small, orange, string bag filled with wooden bricks, and the round spoon we used to eat our midday meal with. Then we lined up as usual to say our last prayer, before we started on our way home. I found it difficult to put my hands together as it was the custom to do, because of the toys and the spoon in my hands. I was a girl who always needed some time to sort myself out. On that day the children had to wait until I had put the string of my bag around my wrist and tucked the spoon into the bag, and while doing this I looked up at sister Festa expecting her to say: Oh, Lisa, come on, you are holding us all up again! Not this time, for as I looked at her, I saw big tears running down her cheeks. When she saw me looking at her, she quickly wiped them away. I felt really guilty, as I thought this time I had become just too much for her. I stopped messing around at once and said: "Es tut mir leid." ("I am sorry."). Still feeling full of guilt, I arrived home and told mother that I had made sister Festa cry, because of my messing about with my bag of toys and spoon before going home. Then mother explained to me the real reason why sister Festa was crying. I was so relieved that I had nothing to feel guilty about, that I didn't care about the Party and the Führer; which I didn't understand anyway, however hard mother tried. As it was she didn't do a very good job, because she found it difficult to understand herself. It would have been difficult for anybody to explain to a five year old a situation which by now even adults found difficult to understand.

It was difficult for most people in Ismaning to understand why it was necessary to remove the sisters from the convent, as they knew the families in the village and had cared for the children ever since most people could remember.

Unterer Anger, the Mother convent in Munich, was founded by Theresia Gerhardinger in 1843, with the help of the Bavarian king, Ludwig I. In 1847 came the call to branch out to America. The King said to the nuns going to America in his fare well speech: "Bleibt Teutsch! Teutsch! Teutsch!" ("Stay German! German! German!" This is how Deutsch was spelled in 1847). He was concerned that the nuns, in emigrating, should not forget their origin and their native language.

The People in Ismaning took pride in their church and the convent at the west side of the church, a high wall separated the church grounds from the convent. For me this was a magical place. A small door in the wall was used by the nuns to attend church services. How I longed to go through this door. But children never went through it. It used to send my imagination soaring sky high. For me it was sheer magic.

After many years living in England when visiting my family in Ismaning, I went to the place where once so proudly stood the convent, next to the old church; this too had gone - a modern church being more desirable. And the wall with the little door had gone as well, and so had the magic.

Once the sisters had left the convent, I too left it. Mother didn't like the idea of a convent without nuns, so consequently I did not go again. I stayed at home until I started school in September 1941.

War!!!!! On 1st September 1939 England declared war on Germany. England had no choice because the German army marched into Poland, and England had a friendship treaty with Poland. Since Adolf Hitler had become Chancellor of Germany he had built up the German army although he was not supposed to have an army according to the treaty of Versailles, but he was not stopped building up that mighty German army. He had promised the people work, and work they got. One ammunition factory was built after the other. He needed straight roads for lorries to drive fast, so he built the Autobahns. The Nazis became very confident and very noisy. One only had to listen to the radio. People were invited to listen to speech after speech and marching songs. I still remember some totally ridiculous songs, for example: 'Heute gehört uns Deutschland, morgen die ganze Welt, und Denn wir fahren gegen England!' Which, crudely translated, means: 'Today Germany belongs to us, tomorrow the whole world, and then we will go against England!'

One Sunday mother came home from church very much disturbed and very worried, she told father that a rumour was going round that the Nazis were closing all the churches and turning them into cinemas, and people dared not go out at night because Nazis were going round beating up any one they felt like. Father in his calm manner found it somewhat amusing, and smiling he assured mother that it wouldn't come to that. As for people getting beaten up at night that just wasn't true. To which mother had a quick answer.

"You know it happened to Franz."

"Well, that is somewhat different," Father replied. "It was in Munich when he was working at the barracks, at the Adolf Hitler Kaserne, where the Nazis are never far away, but here in the village nobody has been beaten. As for making churches into cinemas, it's just an exaggeration. Just you wait, people will come to their senses. Hitler is a big man now, but soon people will realise that he is not the man for them."

56

Mother wasn't quite as confident, but for the time being, she believed her husband. He was always the calm and farsighted husband she could trust. Certain friends tried to persuade my father to join the Party and his excuse was always the same:

"What could the Nazi Party possibly do with me? I can't hear very well, my education is nothing to talk about, the Nazis have no use for me."

It worked to a certain extent, but not always. Once a keen Party member told him that the Party had already chosen a tree in the Au (the large forest along the river Isar), where they would hang all the communists after they had won the war. Father said nothing, but took Koorby's advice and was careful. He realised that even in a village the Nazis could become dangerous.

To Mother he said:

"How can they possibly think that they can win the war, when they haven't even won over their own people?"

The National Party members became louder and louder, rally followed after rally. The German army had, with ease, marched into the Rheinland. Austria was annexed to Germany, Hitler thought it was his right as they were 'practically German' as it was. Poland was needed: Hitler and his Nazis needed Lebensraum (room to live) and plenty of it. Hitler had a very good propaganda minister, Dr. Joseph Göbbels, the Bavarians had a nick name for him, they called him 'De Hupfat Gois' - the limping goat; it was mainly people who did not favour the Nazi Party, but felt that by now it was too late to show it.

*Sister Maria Festa,
leading Kindergarten Sister,
on her 100th birthday*

Chapter Fourteen

Shorsh has a dream.
Father has doubts.
Toni is declared fit for duty.
Toni and his bicycle in the ditch.
Toni and his charm.

Shorsh, my oldest brother, had a dream and this time he didn't want a new pair of boots, he wanted to go to college to become a master carpenter, after he had worked a year as a journeyman. Well, Hitler had other ideas and Shorsh had to obey.

On 18th August 1940, he was enlisted in the Reichsarbeitsdienst, this was work all young people had to do after school or training (In English: Work duty for the Reich). Every teenager had to do this duty for one year, but Shorsh was never permitted to finish his year. Instead, on 2nd December 1940, he was conscripted into the army, in the 4th Infantry Ersatz Battalion 19, in Munich, and with him his friend Hans Lupperger, who was always called Fischer Hans. Those two hoped very much they could stay together, but it was not to be. Shorsh was sworn into the army on 13th December 1940 and was trained in the armoury, in using the Karabiner 98 (standard German infantry rifle), in the Adolf Hitler Kaserne, so called because Hitler was stationed there before WW1. My parents were devastated; father so well remembered the days when he was a soldier in the German Wehrmacht (army) in the First World War. He hated being a soldier and hated the war. Then there was Toni, his youngest son, what would happen to him? Would they take him too? That thought was unbearable for him. And then there was a nagging thought at the back of his mind: Would his sons have to go to war if he had joined the Nazis? Mother soon tried to put that idea out of his mind, as she tried to convince him otherwise when she said:

"Look here, even if you had joined the Party you would not be important enough to keep your sons out of the army."

Yet, this question remained in father's mind. Would it have made a difference? It might just have made a difference, mightn't it? Well, that father would never know and now it was too late.

On 20th June 1940, Toni was declared fit for duty by the medical officer at the Ersatz Battalion R.19, in Munich. He had to report for duty on 4th February 1941 and was sworn into the army on 22nd February 1941. Although he had finished his training as a bricklayer, he had not yet taken his final exam to become a journeyman, therefore by special permission he took this exam in the army, and passed.

My parents, already deeply saddened by the fact that their eldest son had had to leave for the army, were completely heartbroken when it was time for their youngest son to say good-bye. Toni saw how devastated his parents felt and as he shook Father's hand he said:

"Don't worry about us, you'll see before long, we'll both come through that door again." It was a quick kiss for mother and a ruffling of my hair as he reminded me: "Watch those teeth of yours, don't forget to clean them."

A few days before, his girlfriend had given me a tooth brush which I was not so keen on using, yet on that day I assured him that I would use it regularly, then a quick kiss and he was out of the door. Suddenly it was so still in the house, not a sound was to be heard, it was an eerie feeling. Father stood at the door looking at Toni as long as he could see him. He gripped the doorframe so hard that his knuckles went white. He kept saying: "Not my boys - let me keep my boys."

Mother sat on a chair by the table crying quietly and saying: "Mother of God, look after my boys, please, look after my boys."

I crept onto her lap, put my arms around her neck and cried too, I didn't know why I cried, I just cried because she did. Never had I seen my parents so despairing.

Both my brothers were very good-looking. Tall, blond and blue-eyed, just as Hitler wanted his soldiers, but neither of them was striving to get ahead in the army. They both had a trade, and in that they wanted to get ahead. Toni was always funny, daring and somewhat cheeky. Whereas Shorsh was serious and problems seemed to follow him however hard he tried to avoid them. Toni with his cheek and charm didn't go through problems; he managed to walk around them. In the barracks in Munich he found it very hard that he should be so near home, and yet, he could not go home when he wanted. He was the one who never wanted to go away from home.

Sometimes, when it was easy, he jumped over the fence and on an old bicycle, which he had hidden in a ditch, he rode home. His friends used to cover for him. It was to their benefit as well, as he brought parcels back from their parents. With Toni was our cousin Sepp and Fischer Hans, who had since childhood been a close friend of Shorsh, and they both hoped that they could stay together. But this was not to be. Fischer Hans had to join Toni now, the younger brother of the two and then there was Ludwig Knott, from Schleissheim, near Munich. They all became good friends and stayed friends even after the war. For our parents, Toni's escapades were a great worry, although very pleased to see him, but every time they prayed he wouldn't get caught. He never did, but then he wasn't all that long in the barracks.

Yet Toni's charm didn't always come up trumps, especially when it was his turn to clean their barrack. A young officer came to inspect it and asked: "Who cleaned this dormitory?"

Toni proudly announced: "I did." As he thought that he had done a really good job, and probably would be praised. The officer looked into the ash tray under the iron stove and found a little ash in it, pulled it out and emptied the ashes on the floor, spreading them around as much as he could. The soldiers stood there looking at him, nobody said a word. The officer then started quite clearly to feel uncomfortable, said to Toni: "Just clear it up." And quickly left the barrack.

Most officers were Prussians, which very often was the cause of friction. The soldiers were not permitted to speak the strong Bavarian dialect. But somehow they usually got around that, to the annoyance of the officers. This happened quite frequently during class when learning how to handle a specific weapon. I remember one incident Shorsh much later told me. They were still all together, but in different barracks, and in training lessons all the soldiers were together. In one such lesson, after a rifle drill, Fischer Hans, well known for his dry humour, was asked to explain how to fit the barrel. He tried his hardest to speak High German, but managed to do this with a strong Bavarian accent. The class was in stitches and the officer couldn't even say anything, as Hans did try to speak High German, albeit with a Bavarian accent. Well, they still had some fun, but of course it couldn't possibly last.

Chapter Fifteen

Shorsh is moved to Poland.
Hitler breaks the friendship pact with Russia.
The Eastern Campaign.
The internment camp for Jewish people.
Newsflashes come thick and fast.
Mother doesn't listen to newsflashes any more.

On 14th April 1941 Shorsh had to join the occupying forces in the Ostraum, East Poland. Some of the soldiers had an idea or were merely guessing, a young soldier from the Rhineland said to Shorsh: "We are going against Russia, you'll see."

Shorsh tried to reassure him and himself when he said:

"Never! Just look, there are still trains going by. Germany is still trading with Russia, they are still sending coal and grain to Germany. Besides, Germany has a non-aggression pact with Russia, no way are we going into Russia."

Pete, the young man from the Rhineland couldn't be dissuaded, he was visibly afraid and he was right. Since when did a non-aggression pact ever stop Hitler?

On 14th May in the morning, at 4 o'clock when the soldiers got up they saw that the lookout towers on the Russian border had gone. Shorsh asked what had happened, but none of the soldiers could tell him, but they soon knew. From 15th May 1941 until June 21st the troops were prepared for the Eastern Campaign, they were going into Russia! In February 1941 Franz Mösl, who lived with his family on the first floor in my parent's house, received his draft papers and after his training in the barracks in Munich he too had to join the Eastern Campaign.

On the way to the Polish-Russian border, between Legionowo and Modlin, in the forest, the German troops passed an internment camp for Jews: men, women and children of all ages. The soldiers had strict orders not to go near them. Later when Shorsh met some soldiers who came after the first troops, he enquired about those people as he was concerned and was told that they had all been shot. The barbarity of it all broke his heart. Shorsh's letters still arrived, although somewhat infrequently now, but still they did arrive, sometimes dirty and creased with just a few words scribbled on them, but they told my parents that he was all right.

One of our neighbours was very enthusiastic about the regime and whenever there came a newsflash on the radio and there came many, announcing the advancing of the German troops, he came with a large map to show my father the exact location of the German troops in Russia. He had no idea how painful and heartbreaking it was for my parents, for they knew very well how heavy and bloody those battles in Russia were. Sometimes on my way home from school at midday, the neighbour's wife would call from her window:

"Quickly Lisa, run home, a newsflash has been announced, tell your mama."

When I did tell my mother she didn't turn on the radio but said instead: "She'll listen for both of us."

It was mostly propaganda anyway. Dr. Göbbels was very busy.

Shorsh's battalion marching into Poland.
Shorsh took his glove off
so that we could recognise him in the photo.

My Brother, Shorsh 1941

Chapter Sixteen

My Brother Shorsh in the Russian Campaign, WW2.

Shorsh had been trained to mount the machine gun and in the infantry his special task was to carry the gun carriage on his back, but because of that he did not have to carry his own rifle.

On 22nd June – until 10th July 1941 the German troops were heavily engaged in a double battle near Bialystok and Minsk.

1) 22nd June to 24th June, breakthrough through the border position.
2) Battle of Bialystok-Slonim.

From 11th July until 31st July 1941, Shorsh was in another bloody battle near Smolensk. Here he got separated from Pete the 19 year old, who, since the German troops marched into Poland was with Shorsh, so he went looking for him and found him - he had half his head blown off. Shorsh took off his dog tag, gave it to the officer in charge who then called for volunteers to bury the dead. Shorsh always volunteered and so did others, who performed this last task for their comrades quietly and exhausted.

1) 11th July until 15th July was called by the Germans 'Clearing the space south and east and west of Minsk'. Which meant anybody living there was transported to labour camps in Germany.
2) 16th July until 19th July 1941, a three day nightmarish march began from the Berezina to the Dnieper, both big rivers in Russia.

The heat and dust were unimaginable and no rest. Every so often one of the soldiers fell down, having fallen asleep, and was pulled up again by his comrades. How did they do it, marching in full uniform, carrying their rifles and rucksacks on their backs. Shorsh had to carry the heavy gun carriage on his back. On the third day of marching they all had run out of water and to say that they were extremely thirsty is an understatement. They came to a pond, the water was stagnant, the officers run ahead waving the soldiers off trying to stop them from drinking as the risk of the water being poisoned was great. Yet with the state those soldiers were in they didn't care whether they lived or died. They just overrun the officers and drunk as much water as they wanted and not one soldier became sick, and still no rest. The march continued and at last it ended in a wood near the Dnieper, where they found a few deserted houses with straw roofs. That night Shorsh was not on guard duty and all he could think about was sleep. He dug himself a hole with his little spade, pulled off some straw from one of the deserted houses, lined his hole with that straw, took off his jacket crawled into the hole and covered himself with his jacket and fell immediately fast asleep. He slept until dawn, when the sun started to come up. He sat up in his hole and for some seconds he thought he was dreaming. Most of the trees around their camp had lost their crowns with only their trunks pointing to the sky. Wounded and dead soldiers were lying around, so he asked one of the soldiers helping the paramedics: "What happened?"

The soldier didn't think he was hearing right. He looked at Shorsh in utter disbelief asking:

"Did you not hear it? The Russians pounded us all night with the artillery and all we could do was dig holes as fast as we could, but most of us were not quick enough."

It was all so horrific and he could not understand that he hadn't heard it and for a moment he thought that he might have been hit, but he could stand up and felt alright. Then came the task of collecting the dog tags and handing them over to the officers, so that their families could be informed.

Then the troops gathered together - only to march into another battle.

1) From 20th July until 31st July 1941, followed the battle near Mohilev
2) From 29th July until 31st July 1941, the German troops advanced over the Szosh River and into another battle.

The war was relentless, the Russian defence was harder and harder to overcome, also the partisans became more successful.

From 1st August until 8th August 1941, the troops went into battle near Roslavl.

From 9th August until 20th August 1941, battle at Krychaw and Gomel (called 'Extermination battle at Klimowitschi and Miloslawitschi')

From 20th August until 1st October 1941 followed the defensive battles near Yelnya
and Smolensk.

It was here where it was his duty for 3 weeks to fetch the food supply for the company from the field kitchen to the front. He did that in the night when he could go by the light of the stars, and it was less hot. But he was terrified every night that perhaps he might meet a Russian soldier or get caught by partisans. He was glad when his 3 weeks were over, and he was still alive.

From 28th August until 6th September 1941
   a) Defensive battles in the Yelnya-Curve
   b) Defensive battles on the Desna River

2nd October 1941 until 3rd October 1941, double battle near the Vyazma River and Bryansk

3rd October until 4th October 1941, breakthrough through the Desna position

5th October until 13th October 1941, advance over Bolva and Ugra.

At home in Ismaning, by now food was rationed, although we didn't go hungry yet and propaganda was sill in full swing. Newsflashes proclaimed that the German troops would soon enter Moscow. Then it was announced in the news to help the war effort people at home had permission to send warm clothing to the Russian front as the soldiers were not sufficiently equipped for the extreme cold. My mother lost no time in preparing a large parcel with warm clothes for

Shorsh. Right in the middle of it she put the biggest apple from our apple tree and some handkerchiefs. She knew her sons always needed handkerchiefs. Anni, who still lived with her two children upstairs and was very courageous, took the packet to the main post office in Munich, which was the collection point. The packet was rather large and mother was worried it might not be accepted. So far, only one food parcel a month was permitted and the weight was not to exceed one kilogram. But Anni came home absolutely bubbling with excitement, when she told mother that the clerk didn't ask any questions, neither did he weigh it, and best of all she exclaimed, the clerk didn't even look at her, just took the packet and threw it on the heap with all the others and attended to the next customer. Now my mother also got quite excited, as she knew what Anni was thinking: if it was that easy, then the same could be done with a food parcel. Mother started baking, and Anni hopped on her bicycle, went to shops in the village to buy some biscuits and anything else she could get without a ration card. Most shopkeepers were only too pleased to help. The next day Anni again went to Munich to the main post office and exactly the same happened again. The clerk took the parcel and threw it with all the others. Those two women were absolutely elated and so was father, as he most of all knew how hard food was to come by on the front.

Chapter Seventeen

My parents don't hear from Shorsh.
He receives both parcels.
He doesn't have enough time to write.
Stalin's Organ; a weapon from Hell.

Shorsh had received both packages; the handkerchiefs and the apple were welcome. The apple was frozen solid, he defrosted it over a bunker light and thought manna from heaven couldn't taste better. But he had enough warm clothes, the used handkerchief from his pocket he put into the package, closed it again and sent it back home. To his surprise and delight, two days afterwards, he received the food parcel. He and his friends had a feast, but no respite.

13th October until 4th December 1941 - advance towards Moscow and Voronezh.

13th October 1941 until 26th October 1941 - breakthrough through the Moscow defence, capture of Vereya.

27th October until 4th December 1941 - battles to the west of Moscow.

5th December until 21st December 1941- defensive battle 60 km before Moscow - that is as far as the German troops advanced.

22nd December 1941 until 3rd January 1942 - again defensive battles in the Nara-Moskwa-Russa position. The German troops never reached Moscow; the Russian defence was too strong.

On 26th October 1941, when the German troops captured Vereya, Shorsh and his company arrived at a small village where a few Russian civilians were still living in wooden houses. They surprisingly showed the German soldiers great kindness. The soldiers had an opportunity to wash themselves - this was very rare. Shorsh really appreciated this, as he was terribly plagued by lice. He was standing in a house by the window and heard a peculiar noise - it wasn't the noise of a shot being fired. At first he thought it might have been the noise of lightening, but no thunder.

Then he thought perhaps it was a Fieseler Storch (Fieseler Stork) a small German liaison aircraft built by Fieseler before, during, and after WW2.

Then it was suddenly quiet. He threw himself on the floor, against the outside wall, thinking he might have a chance to survive in case the house collapsed. But while he was still throwing himself on the floor they were hit. It was total devastation. Then they knew that they were hit by Stalin's Organ. They had heard of it, but now they had experienced it. Stalin's Organ was not one weapon, but many. It was about 12 or 14 rockets, which could be launched simultaneously from a truck. Their firing range was not very great, but where it hit, the ground shook. Fifty percent of the company were dead. It was gruesome: soldiers without arms or legs. Then volunteers were asked to bury their comrades, which was an impossibility. The Russian winter had already started it was snowing and the ground was frozen solid. With the small spades the soldiers had they couldn't even make an indentation in the ground, let alone dig a grave. All they could do was put them together and cover them with snow.

One soldier asked: "Where did it come from?"

"Right out of hell." Was one suggestion, and he was not far wrong. The soldiers nick-named it Stalin's Organ because of the swishing noise it made when those rockets were launched as some thought it sounded like the bellows of an organ. That night Shorsh was on guard duty for one hour, this was usual, every soldier had to do one hour. In that hour Shorsh smoked 4 cigarettes. Every cigarette took just over 10 minutes and after the fourth cigarette Shorsh knew his guard duty was all but over. While he was standing guard, another company far away was singing the marching song Es war ein Edelweiss (It was an Edelweiss). After that he found it difficult to listen to that song. There he was amidst all the dead and heavily wounded, and that song would never let him forget it. The next day troops got ready to march again towards Moscow. On the way they passed a Sanka (German Field Ambulance) which had been taking wounded soldiers back to a field hospital. They had been ambushed by the partisans and shot.

Chapter Eighteen

1st December 1941. There are no postmen in Ismaning, only post women.
My parents have no news from Shorsh.
Miracles do happen!

On 1st December 1941, the troops were engaged in defensive battles to the west of Moscow, trying to retreat. Shorsh was standing behind a tree and suddenly fell down, quickly he tried to get up again, but couldn't manage, he felt something warm on his left thigh and he knew that he was hit. He called for a Sanitäter (paramedic) and felt somebody reaching under his arms, pulling him, before he lost consciousness. His left hip was shot through and so was his sciatic nerve. At home my parents were nearly beside themselves with worry. By now they had two sons in the war. Toni's letters still arrived, but nothing from Shorsh. The package with warm clothing came back with a used handkerchief right in the middle, the apple was gone. Somebody had clearly opened it; the whole thing was a puzzle. Every morning mother watched for the post woman, all postmen had joined the army, yet no letter from Shorsh. Toni's letters arrived not too often, but they did arrive. Then came Christmas 1941 and no news from Shorsh. On Boxing Day, Christmas came to my parents. Anni, who lived with her two children in our house, had been recruited to deliver the mail. Every day she went through the post and nothing from Shorsh. But on Boxing day, although it was not a normal day for postal delivery, Anni still went to work, went through the post and came home waving a card, which was sent by a paramedic from Vereya, saying: Shorsh is alive, but badly wounded in his leg, but will survive. What a present this was for my parents! Now they really could celebrate Christmas, as far as this was possible.

In the main treatment station in Vereya, the shrapnel from his leg had been removed. He was in excruciating pain and kept shouting: "Take my boot off!" Even though he didn't have any boots on, but he still had the feeling that he was wearing one, thinking if they'd only take it off, the pain would go. After he had been patched up in Vereya he was transported with a Panja Wagon (small wooden cart pulled by horses, for three or perhaps four wounded soldiers) to Obrobka. When they arrived at Obrobka, on every telephone mast hung a soldier. Shorsh didn't know if they were Germans or Russians. They were too traumatised to see any difference. All they could see were soldiers hanging there. The field hospital in Obrobka could not by any stretch of the imagination be called a hospital. The only building still complete was the train station and that had to do for a hospital. The hall was divided into two rooms by a tarpaulin. One part served as an operating theatre and the other part served as a ward. The concrete floor was covered with straw and had to be used instead of beds. Here again Shorsh was plagued by lice and used a little stick to scratch himself, wherever he could reach. Paramedics went through the so-called hospital with limbs in their hands, taking them outside, probably to dispose of them. Shorsh was in so much pain that caring about anything was beyond him. From Obrobka he was transported to Lowitsch near Warsaw. It was here where, for the first time since he was injured, he felt the luxury of a real war hospital with nurses and doctors around him.

Where my parents had been beside themselves with worry, they were now beside themselves with happiness. Shorsh was alive and in time would come home. What could be better?

A few months later Benedict Off, yes, the one whom everybody in Ismaning called Off Beni and who gave Toni, my younger brother, the Flobert which he blew up in our garden, came to see my parents when he came home on leave. My parents, although pleased to see him, found it somewhat surprising when he asked if Shorsh had survived.

"Oh, yes," they said. "He was badly wounded, but will recover and is in a war hospital near Warsaw."

Then Off Beni told them a most extraordinary story. As I mentioned before, he too was on the Russian campaign and in the horrific battle to the west of Moscow, where for some unknown reason he got separated from his unit. He had heard someone shouting for the paramedic, but no paramedic was near so he ran to the soldier who was shouting and gripped him under his arms and pulled him away, towards the paramedic. He recognised Shorsh, but by then Shorsh was already unconscious, so didn't know that it was Off Beni who gripped him under his arms and pulled him away from the tree. When Beni got Shorsh to the paramedic he said: "Try to get him through, he lives in my road."

To which the paramedic replied very dryly: "But of course, I perform miracles all the time."

And just as dryly Beni answered: "All right, you can perform one here then."

He then left Shorsh, as he had to find his unit.

To my parents he said: "I have no idea how I got separated from my unit, but on second thought, it wasn't really surprising. Everybody was running, trying to get cover while the Russians were bombarding us with their artillery. We've had it, I thought. We will never get to Moscow now."

Father shook his head in agreement, and said: "You never had a chance. Hitler isn't the first one to have had that crazy idea."

Off Beni had to agree with him, and just nodded his head.

"I'm so glad Shorsh survived, I had my doubts," he said. "Tell him to give a kiss to one of the pretty nurses from me."

That was Off Beni, always a little humour tucked away somewhere in his heart. Shorsh and Off Beni never met again, because Off Beni was killed in action on 22nd January 1945.

Zum Andenken ✠ im Gebete

an unſeren lieben, unvergeßlichen, herzensguten
Gatten, Vater, Sohn, Bruder, Schwiegerſohn,
Schwager und Onkel

Benedikt Off

von Iſmaning / Stabsgefr. in einem Inf.-Regt.

Feldzugsteilnehmer geg. Polen, Frankreich, Rußland
Inhaber des Verwundetenabzeichens, des Kriegs-
verdienſtkreuzes 2. Kl. m. Schw. und der Oſtmedaille

Geboren am 15. Mai 1915 in Billingsdorf
gefallen am 22. Januar 1945 in Ungarn.

O weinet nicht ihr Teuren,
Mein junges Leben iſt vollbracht.
Ich hab den Tod gefunden in heißer blutiger Schlacht,
Ich hab' auch empfangen den größten Siegeslohn,
Der dem ſterbenden Krieger iſt verheißen —
Es iſt die Himmelskron.
O tröſtet Euch Gattin, Eltern und Kinder,
im fernen Heimattal,
Wir treffen uns ja wieder im ſchönen Himmelsſaal.
Und klingt in der Heimatkirche für mich
der Glocken Trauerton.
So blickt mein Heldenauge auf Euch herab
N-0316 vom Himmelsthron.

In loving memory of a precious hero,
Benedikt Off, 'Off Beni'

Chapter Nineteen

News flashes gradually stop.
September 1941 I start school.

Listening to the English broadcasts in the evenings was strictly prohibited. Anybody listening could be detected and imprisoned or worse. But people still broke this law.

Once the troops advancing on Moscow started to retreat, newsflashes stopped. The German people were not permitted to know that the advance to Moscow was unsuccessful and what's more, how many soldiers lost their lives. To listen to any foreign radio station was against the law and punished with imprisonment or worse, and yet people still kept breaking it, especially parents whose sons were on the front. My parents also broke this law. I was usually in bed when the English broadcast in German was announced on the radio, because that was the only way they could learn where the front was. My cot was in the master bedroom in the corner on the right from the door with the head pushed against the wall, where on the other side of the wall the Volksempfänger (literally "people's receiver" - the only make of radio available) stood on a table in the living room. So however low they turned the dial on the radio I still could hear the signature tune, which was the start of Beethoven's 5th symphony. That boom-boom-boom boom was still audible for me, and to this day I cannot understand why it had to be so loud. I knew my parents were not supposed to listen to this broadcast and that really worried me terribly. Then I told my mother that I could hear the signature tune when I was in bed. She was very surprised at this unexpected announcement and quite shocked and told me not ever to tell anybody and I promised that I wouldn't, but I wanted to listen too. So they let me stay up and I too was allowed to listen, needless to say I didn't understand any of it. Father tried to explain it to me, I found it all very boring and after a while I didn't want to stay up any more, but I understood why they broke the law. Toni was still out there somewhere and it was called the front where he was fighting - whom?

"The Russians." father told me.

"Where was he?" Came my next question.

"Well," father replied with a heavy heart, "He is in a country called Finland very far in the north, where it is very cold and sometimes he is very hungry, that's why your mother is always sending parcels."

I was an inquisitive child, with a logic of my own and asked: "If it is so bad why doesn't he stop fighting the Russians and come home?"

Mother started to cry and father hugged me as he tried to explain to me a question they found hard to explain to themselves.

"You know, the Führer, Herr Hitler, told him to do it."

By then I had learned not to ask questions about the Führer. I had learned a very hard lesson on that.

Many years later, when I already lived in England, I met a Danish Lady who told me that her father used to listen to the English news in the evening and that she used to stand in the road looking out for the detector van, to be able to quickly run into the house to tell her father who then had enough time to switch off the radio. But fortunately to her relief the detector van never appeared.

In September 1941, I started school. In my years in the kindergarten it was our natural thinking that when we went to school it was the sisters who would teach us, but in 1941 it was a Fraulein (young lady) who taught us. She was a pretty young lady and wore a flowery dress made of muslin the first day I went to school. She was a good teacher, but I don't think she liked me a lot. I talked too much and the conversation didn't always go in the right direction. We heard a great deal about the life of our glorious Führer when he was a very young man before he became our great leader. How he had to struggle, that he only had a room in the Mansarde (attic) and had only bread and milk to eat. For the life of me I could not understand that that should be such a hardship. In our house we had two rooms we called Mansarde, they were perfectly good rooms, they just had a slanting ceiling, and I loved bread and milk. So, what was all that about? Then I said:

"Well, that is not so bad, Jesus often didn't have that, he often didn't even have a bed to sleep in and nobody says anything about that anymore."

The silence that followed was deafening, immediately I knew I had committed a major offence. I wasn't exactly sure what it was that I shouldn't have said and the exact offence I was never told, but I had to write 20 times, I must not have a big mouth.

She then asked me: "Can you count up to 20?"

"Of course I can, Sister Festa taught us."

I was really digging myself a hole there, first I talked about Jesus and then I said that a nun taught me. Actually, it was not Sister Festa but my parents, but in the whole confusion I didn't know anymore who had taught me what. At the time I didn't understand any of it. All the things we heard about our Führer, I had no idea what a Führer was. But I came to learn that it was the man in the picture above the teacher's desk, where once had been a cross. Now every morning we prayed to the Führer.

Chapter Twenty

Die Strasse der Gebirgsjäger - The road of the mountaineers.
Soldiers and Artists.
The three friends.
Home on leave (the only time).

Toni, Sepp our cousin and their friend Fisher Hans, and
Ludwig Knott from Munich, joined on 12th August 1941 the
Feld Ersatz Battalion 1047 (Field Reserve Battalion 1047)
and so far they had been able to stay together, and together
they were transferred on 22nd August 1941 until 27th
September 1941 to occupy Norway, which was taken over by
the German forces on 9th June 1940. The boys had a
wonderful time and thought Norway was beautiful. To their
delight they had permission to swim in the fjords, the water
was crystal clear and diving in from the rocks above was a
huge amount of fun, but it was war and the duration of those
pleasures were very short. On 28th September until 13th
October 1941 the troops were used to protect the coast of
Norway, which they continued to occupy until 30th October
1941. Then from 10th November until 18th December the
Marschbattalion 1047 came under the command of Major
General Eduard Dietl, and became the Gebirgsjägerregiment
139, 13 Kompanie (Mountaineer Regiment 139, 13th
Company). General Dietl was a Bavarian, and most of the
Mountaineers were Bavarians and Austrians and when those
young men were conscripted they were told:

"You are Bavarian," (or as it was Austrians) "You can
ski, so you are going to Finland." Whether they could
actually ski did not come into the equation. To Toni's delight
he was allocated to be adjutant to the officer Count Max
Khevenhüller von Metsch, in the region of Niederosterwitz,
in Laundsdorf, Austria. Bavarians and Austrians understand
each other, as they are so much alike. It was lucky for Toni to
end up working for an Austrian Officer. Max Khevenhüller
was always able to recognise Toni's tendency towards
indiscipline and managed to reign him in before there were
any serious consequences. The relationship of the two men
was always that of friends rather than that of officer and
adjutant.

1st January to 14th January 1942, the battle for the position at the Wermanabschnitt, near Alakurtti, in North Finland.

15th January 1942 the troops advanced to North Finland.

Germany had a friendship pact with Finland. Together they fought against Russia. How unbelievable it must have seemed for these young soldiers to fight a winter war at 30 or 40 degrees below zero Centigrade in the Arctic Circle, between the Eismeerstrasse and das Weisse Meer (The White Sea). Although in the Western hemisphere, for the mountaineers it seemed like a different planet.

There, in the far North, the young soldiers had to get used to a different kind of war to the war they had been trained to fight in the barracks.

The letters from home kept repeating the questions: How do you live under those conditions? How do you cope with the winter in the arctic, the forests and the marshes, and the days without nights in the summer?

A young soldier and artist, Kurt Kranz, managed to portray with modest means, the life of the soldiers. Home for them was now the Karelian Jungle. And when Kurt Kranz came back to the bunker from guard duty or ski reconnaissance, he remembered the surroundings of snow and ice. With great success he managed, with only a pencil, to put those images on paper. His friends in the bunker never failed to admire his drawings, especially when in the twilight the soldiers could experience the cold magic of the Northern lights. Kurt Kranz managed to capture in 38 drawings a life of incredible harshness, on a unique front, in the winter of the Karelian jungle in Lapland.

On a few rare occasions a friend of Toni, Sepp and Fischer Hans would come home on leave and would then visit the parents of the three friends. They usually told the parents that their sons were very well. Although the parents knew that their sons wanted their friends to say that. But they were still delighted to see any friend of their son, especially as they could send food parcels back with them, as normally they could only receive one kilo per month. One extra kilo of food was very welcome in the arctic. Parents found it very difficult to imagine that their sons had to fight a war under those conditions, where the supply of food was always short.

In spring 1942, the German soldiers started to build a road right through the Karelian jungle to make it possible for transport to follow the troops and to reach Murmansk on the Russian border, which was the aim of the German forces.

Most of the soldiers were very young and many of them had barely finished their training when the conscription papers came through the door. They had no chance to use their professional skill; they had to learn a different skill, one they did not choose. Now between battles they even learned to build a road. Along this road when they had a few days of rest, rest was not what they did. Instead of destroying, they wanted to create. They competed building log cabins. The group Toni was in received first prize, how proud those soldiers were, although they could only sleep two nights in them before they had to move on. They also carved a road sign and to show how proud they felt of their achievements they called this road Die Strasse der Gebirgsjäger (The road of the Mountaineers) and one artistic Mountaineer started to write this name on the road sign, but time was short and the company had to move out again, but this mountaineer could not bear to leave his work half finished, so he stayed behind and finished it and had then to run and catch up with his company.

Alas, those days were too few. War has a habit of catching up with soldiers, however young they are.

4th May 1942, the German troops started to make preparations for the deployment in Kiestinki

5th May 1942, moving out on lorries to Kiestinki, a move of 103 km.

6th May 1942 until 23rd May 1942, offensive battle at Kiestinki.

24th May until 31st May, new pursuit of the retreating Russian troops.

1st June 1942 came the relief of the Finnish battalion, south of the heights of the Njato-wara Mountain.

Until 20th July 1942, heavy battles with artillery.

20th July, the Mountaineers were relieved by the artillery company and continued with building the Road of the Mountaineers.

On 3rd August 1942 the Mountaineers succeeded in capturing the heavily defended Igelstellung position (Hedgehog position) at the foot of the Njato-wara, north of lake 506 with hand-to-hand combat.

On 7th August 1942 followed a march of 3.5 km back to the next bivouac and until 13th August 1942, preparations for the offensive of the Russian stronghold.

14th August 1942 Mountaineer Company 13 prepared to be the first troops at the south of the Njato-wara, but this did not result in a battle as in the meantime the Russian troops had retreated. Instead the reconnaissance squadron on the North Slope of the Njato-wara was relieved.

23rd August 1942, 103 km march and then by lorry through Kuusamo and Märkjärvi and from there transport by railway to the Werman Abschnitt.

1st September 1942 the mountaineers arrived in Wotja and moved into a bivouac at the Nordweg (Northway).

4th September 1942, transport of the Mountaineers to Joutsijärvi.

5th September moving into bivouac in Joutsijärvi and rebuilding of the Mountaineer's camp.

On 19th September 1942 until 10th October Toni and Sepp, our cousin, came home on the only holiday they ever had in the duration of the war. This was a wonderful and unique opportunity for Toni to visit Shorsh. Shorsh had been transported to Berlin in January 1942 where he learned that his next destination would be Koblenz, on the Mosel; from there he was told that the next stop was Cochem, also on the Mosel, this time a hospital on the first floor above a mental asylum. In February 1942 he was moved yet again to a war hospital called Kemperhof, in Koblenz and at the end of February 1942 he was moved into another war hospital called Josefshaus, and the nurses there were Nuns, to Shorsh's dismay, as they were very pretty. From there he was moved to a war hospital in Engers, near Neuwied, on the Rhine. Here Doctors tried a unique operation on Shorsh's hip; they actually tried to join his severed sciatic nerve back together. What an ambitious try it was, if it only had worked! It was also in Engers where Shorsh met his girlfriend, who later became his wife.

In Engers Toni could visit Shorsh for a few days, precious days they were indeed. Those precious days went much too quickly. After all, there was a war on and war has neither the time nor the feeling for sentimentality. Far too soon came the 10th October 1942 and Toni and Sepp had to say good-bye to parents and friends. But nothing was ever straight forward where Toni was involved. They had to catch a train from Munich Hauptbahnhof (main train station) to Danzig (now Gdansk), and from there to Reveil. They both had a pass to be on leave until 10th October 1942. Once on the train, Toni had the brilliant idea to leave it again at the next stop. At once they both went to the officer on duty and told him that the train was so overfilled that they had to get off. With the medley of soldiers coming and going on the station the officer was so busy that he couldn't really spend time on them, so he just stamped their passes and ordered them to take the next train. Because they had their passes stamped by an officer they went into town and had a good time and took the next train the next day. As it worked so well the first time they tried the same thing several times after that. Eventually they arrived at the Port of Reveil, which then still belonged to Germany, but belongs now to Poland. Here they started looking for their ship to go to Norway with some other mountaineers, who were also coming back from leave. All the German soldiers had been billeted in the Adolf Hitler Schule. But while they were waiting an officer came out of the Adolf Hitler Schule, went into his car that was standing in the road, but the car wouldn't start, so the two very helpful mountaineers ran over to him offering to give the car a push. The officer gladly accepted, jumped into the car and Toni and Sepp pushed him down the road until the car started. But they didn't go back, just kept on walking and stashed their rucksacks behind a dustbin, had a night in the town and went back to the port the next morning. But in the meantime the ship they were supposed to board had gone. The two of them, alone, had to wait in the Adolf Hitler Schule until enough soldiers had arrived to be transported to Norway. But now the two were kept under observation. When they eventually arrived back at their unit in Finland they were quick to tell a cock and bull story, about what a terrible journey they had had. But when Toni tried to tell the same story to his superior, Earl Max Khevenhüller, it didn't work so well. The Earl knew Toni too well and he quickly stopped him saying:

"Toni, don't tell me. You are here now, but I promise you this will never happen again." He was right too, it never did happen again, but this had nothing to do with his superior, as none of the mountaineers went on leave ever again and that included Earl Max Khevenhüller.

The start of the Road of the Mountaineers

Soldiers clearing the Karelian Jungle to build Road of the Mountaineers

Camp on the Road of the Mountaineers.
Toni on the left playing bowls

Signposts put up by the Mountaineers

Rest in the marshes

1941, battle on the Road of the Mountaineers

On a rare occasion at a respite,
The Mountaineers created a folk festival

Toni wins first prize for his log cabin

*Camp on the
Road of the Mountaineers*

*Soldiers with a puppy
at a log cabin*

Toni in his Mountaineer uniform

Cousin Sepp in his Mountaineer uniform

A selection of drawings by Kurt Kranz

Kurt Kranz – A Self Portrait

Chapter Twenty One

Another winter in the Arctic.
Christmas in the ice.
Deployment on the Fischerhals Front. Then fighting on the
Fischerhals Peninsula.

Another winter was waiting for the Mountaineers in arctic conditions; another deployment, on the Fischerhals Front. The mountaineers now also became the Jagdkompanie 13 (13th Fighter Company).

18th December 1942 - deployment of the Jagdkompanie 13, in Kelloselkä.

21th December 1942 - deployment of the Jagdkompanie 13 in the area of Korja where they moved to their base in the outpost called Alpenveilchen (little alp violet).

This was truly an outpost to challenge the endurance of the soldiers to their limit. Here, regardless of the temperature, every morning the soldiers put on their skis and went 30 or 40 km on reconnaissance into the no-man's-land, between Finland and Russia.

On 24th December 1942 Christmas arrived, even in North Finland. No sleigh bells and no Christmas Carols, plenty of snow though. There they sat huddled in their bunkers with Christmas parcels from home, as the people at home were still permitted to send 1 kilo every month. Most of the soldiers had a parcel and those who hadn't, shared with those who had. Some of them tried to make a joke, only to stop the misery creeping any further. It didn't work. Then Toni couldn't stand it any longer and went out, cut a small fir tree, brought it into the bunker. He took his shoelaces from his ski boots and started decorating the tree. Then all the other mountaineers joined in. Now at last they had a Christmas tree and thought it was wonderfully decorated. And the amazing thing was that suddenly their spirits lifted. They started singing Christmas carols and to their amazement they realised how many carols they did know, asking each other: Do you know this one or that one?

After a while they started talking and laughing, and thought there was still something special about Christmas. After all, they had food parcels they could share. Christmas did come to the mountaineers in 1942 in the arctic winter of Lapland.

War just continues!

On 1st January 1943, the order came to close the camp and to return to Salla, and until 2nd February 1943, the mountaineers, for the first time, received training in skiing and reconnaissance runs. This came after the mountaineers had been skiing and going on reconnaissance runs for more than two years. Yet it was something they could enjoy.

Deployment on Fischerhals front, from 10th February 1943 until 26th January 1944

9th February 1943 the mountaineers travelled by train to Joutsijärvi and departed from Joutsijärvi across Vikka, 42 kilometres along the Eismeerstrasse and then 15 km along the Titowastrasse.

On 13th February 1943 there was an inspection of the march column by the Oberbefehlshaber, General Oberst Dietl (Supreme Commander in Chief, Major General). The Major General had a special affinity for the mountaineers. Most of the mountaineers came from Bavaria and Austria and the Major General was from Bavaria, from Bad Aibling, near Munich. Therefore it was a natural process that he should feel a kind of friendship and perhaps also some protectiveness towards those young men. I know from Toni how much he was respected and it went a little further than that: he was for them a kind of father figure whom they didn't mind following. Toni always thought that this wasn't viewed so generously by the Nazis. For them he was a little too close to the ordinary soldier.

On 2nd February 1943, Generalfeldmarschal (Field Marshal) Schörner came to visit and addressed the troops, as did General Rossi on 6th March 1943.

On 7th March 1943, the Grenadier Regiment 193 was relieved at the ridge of N6M and N6aM.(This time I cannot translate as I don't know what these figures mean, and I was unable to find out).

On 21st February 1943, Ivalo: entrance into XIX - (Geb.) A.K. (here again I am unable to translate.)

On 23rd March 1943, defence from a Russian attack and a successful counter-attack.

At the April 1943 Narviklauf (Narvik Run- this was a competition in skiing, of all the Companies in Narvik.) the company 139 Gebirgsjäger (Mountaineers) took part in the competition of the Reconnaissance Run and a slalom run and managed to take the prizes. Sepp our cousin secured the first prize. It was a Finnish Dagger, presented to him by none other than Major General Eduard Dietl, who flew especially to Narvik to witness this performance of his Mountaineers. Sepp's grandson still has this dagger and also the newspaper cutting that shows the presentation of the dagger by Major Dietl.

Then, fighting on the Fischerhals Peninsula (A peninsula belonging to Russia) in sector Murmansk.

On 2nd June 1943 Company 12 relieved the mountaineers who moved by train to the summer camp III on N4bm.

31st August 1943 - renewed occupation of the ridges N7M, N6M, N6aM.

15th September 1943 - General Schörner came to visit the troops.

18th November 1943 - conclusion of the relief by company 1. The mountaineers moved into the Narviklager and stayed until 26th January 1944.

May 1944, the Mountaineers were moved to Kiestinki.

15th July 1944, renewed assault to open the way to Sennosero with hand-to-hand combat, where the Mountaineers took a mountain of strategic height called Höhe 150 (Height 150) well known to every mountaineer, as this combat was particularly heavy.

4th September 1944, Finland capitulated and the German forces now had to fight the war on their own in Lapland.

The Road of the Mountaineers

Soldiers on the Fischerhals peninsula

Finnish soldiers on the Road of the Mountaineers

Toni's bunker on the Fischerhals peninsula

Mountaineers skiing on the Eismeerstrasse

Troops getting ready for battle on Höhe 150

From left to right:
Unknown, Toni, Fisher Hans, Sepp in Finland

On reconnaissance near Murmansk

Ski race at Salme-ewi near Saloniki,
North Finland

General Dietl inspecting the troops

General Dietl
Enjoying a cup of coffee

*Above: General Dietl presenting a Finnish
Dagger to cousin Sepp for winning the first
prize in the Mountaineer's ski race*

*Below: the Finnish dagger presented to
Sepp by General Dietl*

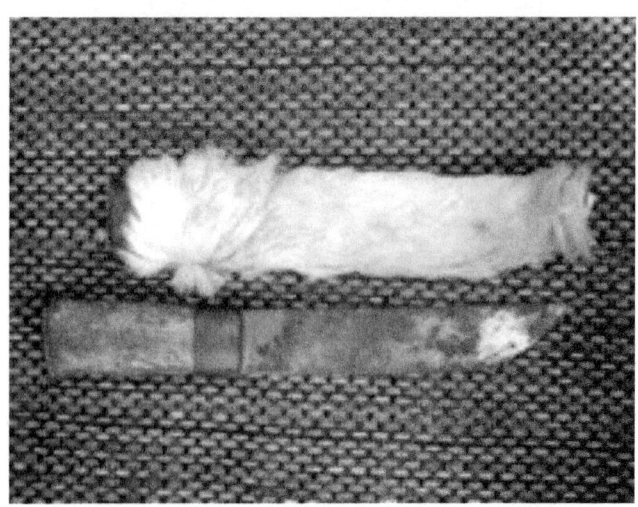

Chapter Twenty Two

What happens in the Fatherland.
Franz comes home on leave.
Shorsh is transferred to a war hospital in Munich called the
Max Gymnasium.
Our 17 year old cousin Rosi is brilliant at dodging hospital
porters.

Early spring 1943, Franz came home on leave for only two weeks from the Russian front. Franz was the young man who lived with his wife Anni and their two children, Anni and Hans, on the first floor in our house. Two weeks he was permitted to live with his family, a dream which lasted but a moment and then it was gone and gone was the life they prayed so hard for. Franz went back to the front and Anni never heard from him again. She received a letter signed by the company commander that Franz was missing in action. What agonising months she had to spend, months of desperate hope, hope he might be alive and perhaps be a prisoner somewhere, then she heard the horrific stories of what the Russians did with their prisoners. Weeks came and went with no word from Franz and the weeks of hope and prayers turned to months, and still Anni would not and could not believe that she would never see her husband again.

In October that unbearably cruel letter from the government came. The post woman on duty gave it to my mother to give to Anni, she wasn't brave enough to do it herself. She knew the letter too well, as she delivered too many of them. Anni just turned and walked away and left my mother to open it. It read that Franz had been missing in action and was, on 12th October, declared as having died bravely for the Fatherland.

In March 1943 Shorsh was transferred to a war hospital in Munich called Max Gymnasium. He still had his whole leg in plaster, which he was banging around with. One couldn't possibly have called it walking, as he had a metal heel inserted in the plaster, which made a terrible banging noise when he was walking.

It was wonderful for all the family to be able to visit him in Munich, but of course visiting hours had to be strictly observed, unless one was as clever and daring as our 17 year old cousin Rosi. She lived with her parents in Munich, on Preising Strasse, and visited Shorsh nearly every day. She was extremely skilled in dodging the porter, who had his little room just inside the entrance door on the right. Rosi used to wait just inside the entrance, out of sight of the porter, and when a member of staff went to the porter with some request, which happened quite frequently, she very quickly slipped by the porter's window and was up the stairs to the first floor where Shorsh had his room. Of course the porter noticed her sometimes and called after her, but she was gone. Well, the porter did his duty in trying to stop her, but he couldn't very well run after her, and Rosi visited Shorsh whenever she wanted to. With Shorsh, four heavily wounded soldiers occupied the room. I particularly remember one young man who was wounded in his head and his sense of direction was disturbed. He was unable to walk straight towards a door, he would arrive to one side of it. Like this it was with everything. He was unable to pick up a cup for instance. He would reach for it to the side of it. Of course his roommates had great fun with him. They used to call his name and throw a cup or something else at him, which of course in the beginning he never caught. This they did as fun until they realised what a marvellous therapy it was. He knew he could not be cured, but he started to adjust. The first thing was that he started to manage to walk through a door; it was wonderful for everybody to see. The Doctors thought that he would be able to adjust completely and that he could live a normal life.

It became increasingly difficult to import food from occupied countries. Grain and coal, the commodities Germany used to import from Russia, had now to be imported from other sources, but as the German front-lines were so widely spread and the infrastructure of German occupied countries was very often destroyed, Germany was to a great deal depending on its own agriculture for food. The food allocated by ration cards was barely enough. By governmental order farmers, and that included smallholdings and even ordinary households, had been compelled to declare everything that was produced. Even live stock had to be declared. And by law everybody had to give up a certain percentage for the war effort. The German people started to get hungry and tried to produce as much as they could themselves. Flower gardens disappeared one by one. Instead gardens were planted with cabbages, potatoes, lettuces or anything else that could be eaten. The Deutsch Mark started to lose its value. Food was the currency one could pay with.

My parents kept chickens and with 30 eggs my mother bought a leather satchel for me from a local saddler. For the first year at school, children still used a slate and a slate pen to write with. As they advanced to higher classes they used wooden penholders with metal nibs that could be pushed into the end. The nibs I used were called Redis Feder, but they didn't last very long and my mother paid three eggs for each nib, she normally bought two. Anni had a source in Munich where she could get stationary, but only when she paid with eggs. This of course needed courage, as it was black market and against the law.

Mother didn't declare her chickens, and so far nobody had paid any attention to them. But they did become a problem when my parents secretly fed a pig in the outhouse. Nobody noticed anything untoward until my parents and Anni slaughtered it. Somebody noticed and told the police, who promptly turned up the following day. It was the police inspector, whom my parents knew, accompanied by a very young ambitious policeman. They told my parents that they knew that they had slaughtered a pig. There was no point in denying it, and with a heavy heart they admitted their crime, which of course meant they had to give it up. They were permitted to keep one kilo, and they even got paid for the rest, but who wanted money? Then the meat was loaded into a car, and as they were about to leave that young ambitious policeman said to my mother:

"I have seen that you have chickens, have you declared them?"

My mother just looked at him, and she absolutely snapped. She had just lost all the meat from her pig and he dared to ask if she had declared her chickens? She went right up to him, looking sinister and in a very quiet and menacing voice she said:

"No, I have not declared my chickens and do you know why not? I have one son in a war hospital after being seriously wounded on the Russian Front, another son in North Finland, do you know where that is? It is very cold up there, and they never get enough food, that is why I send him biscuits, and that is what I do with my eggs. By the way you are about the age of my sons, so why aren't you fighting for your fatherland?"

And with that she poked him with her forefinger in the chest. The inspector looked quite worried and said: "It's alright lady, just declare them when you get round to it."

And with that he ushered the young man through the door, he looked quite bewildered. Then Mother collected herself and rational thinking took over and very troublesome thoughts entered her mind: Surely that young policeman would report her to the Gestapo. And at four or five o'clock in the morning they would come and arrest her. When she told father that evening he thought it was very funny and laughing he said: "You did what?" And still laughing he said: "I would have liked to see a Nazi get poked in the chest by an angry woman."

Mother didn't find that funny and was very cross with Father, but he tried to allay her fears saying: "The inspector would never permit that, he is a good man."

Mother was not entirely convinced, but when a few days had elapsed and no Gestapo appeared she knew that she had got away with it this time. But the fear of the Gestapo never quite left her. Yet she was a stubborn woman, and she never did declare her chickens. She thought if the Nazis found out she would apologise and declare them, but I think that it helped that she had two sons in the army.

I too, received a warning one evening when I was late running home from a friend's, where I had overstayed and knew I would be told off by my mother, as usual. It was a habit of mine to stay out longer than I should have. It was getting dusk and I decided to take a shortcut through the park. I was just coming to the gate at the other end when a man came towards me. It was too dark to recognise him and he didn't recognise me either. I was somewhat nervous and as we passed each other I said, in a very friendly manner: "Goodnight!"

To my surprise it was the Mayor, my father's friend, and it was not surprising that his answer was not Goodnight, but instead he said: "Heil Hitler is the German greeting."

I was so frightened and started running and didn't stop until I ran into my mother's arms at home. Very alarmed she kept asking me what had happened, but my answer took a while in coming as I was completely out of breath and when I told her, Father, who was already home from work, was furious. He was so angry and shouted: "Is that the doctrine of the Party now, that they frighten children?"

The mayor, being a friend of father's, Mother became quite worried that it was not beyond her husband to go and see him to tell him what he thought. As always she managed, with her realistic outlook, to calm her husband with a logic that sometimes escaped Father.

"You know that we all have to use Heil Hitler as a greeting with the right hand raised. That is just as it is and you making a fuss only sends us all where we don't want to go. You know she always forgets to say Heil Hitler; she got into trouble once before at school, her teacher told me that there are some children who just run into the class room without saying Heil Hitler. And turning to me, pointing a finger she said: "And you miss, you say Heil Hitler from now on." I faithfully promised I would.

In her logic mother recognised the reality as she turned to Father and said:

"I know you still think of the Mayor as Koorby your friend, but what would you have him say, a friendly goodnight Lisa. Now that would have made trouble for him. Can't you see that?"

Of course she was right. I didn't forget to say Heil Hitler again. But I did wonder where we would have to go if father shouted too much, but I didn't ask. By now I had learned not to ask about things I didn't understand. Too many times I had heard 'Don't ask, it's got nothing to do with you.' But there was one thing mother had forgotten and it was that children have big ears and mine were X.L. Mother had several friends who used to come for coffee in the afternoon, as is customary in Bavaria. Often they would whisper, thinking that I would not hear. How wrong they were! Now when I am thinking back I wonder how they knew so much. Dachau, a concentration camp near Munich often came up in the conversation and the stories, terrifying stories, made me wish they would not come any more. I was worried about my parents, especially about my father. He worked in Munich at the E.V.M. I could not find out what those letters stood for. As father only ever said E.V.M. It was a large soup kitchen where men and women worked. Since 1942 air raids became more and more frequent and people who had lost everything had no way of obtaining food. Therefore at certain collection points they could at least have something to eat. Food was delivered in lorries by the men who worked at the E.V.M. My father was one of them. They had to work shifts day and night, and at night it was particularly hazardous as air raids still mostly happened at night. Mother was very worried when father had to work at night. Once she said:

"I wonder why you and Schwegler (another friend) always have to do the most dangerous jobs, did you say something to make yourselves unpopular?" At this father laughed loudly:

"Unpopular." He blurted out, "I don't have to say anything, I was unpopular before the whole mess started, besides I am not the only unpopular person there, none of us joined the Party. They would be only too happy if a bomb would drop on us. Do you know what? Right now I wish I knew myself what my opinion was; maybe things would be different if I had joined the Party." "Oh yes," Mother was quick to answer. "I can imagine you keeping quiet and agreeing with everything they say, and do, for that matter. Oh, things would be different, we probably would not be here anymore."

There it was again: Where would we be? I didn't ask. The answer I would get would have been too vague and too confusing or just: It has nothing to do with you. I learnt to work out for myself what was going on, it was not always quite right, but it also was not always far wrong. For one thing I knew my parents were frightened and that frightened me. I learned to observe people and listen to them. There were the bold ones with loud, sharp voices and there were the quiet and timid ones, who were alarmed and frightened. The quiet voices that whispered, I found much more frightening, because those whispered, spine chilling stories had an unbelievable ring to them. There was one story that even at the age of seven I did not believe. And when much later I heard it again I still found it hard to believe. A friend of mother's who came for coffee one afternoon whispered to her that she had heard that the Nazis made lampshades from the skin of the Jews. I still find it difficult to believe.

Rosi, who skilfully managed to
dodge the hospital porters

Chapter Twenty Three

Shorsh goes to college.
Shorsh has to prove his Aryan ancestry.
Shorsh is accused of having attacked a superior officer.
Shorsh is imprisoned in Engers.
Sunday 17th December 1944, a terrific air raid over Munich.

While in the war hospital, the Max Gymnasium, Shorsh went to high school to study Bauzeichner (graphic drawing for buildings) something which was possible to do while at the Max Gymnasium. Then in spring 1943 he was transferred to a rehabilitation hospital, where he learned, as he had successfully completed the Bauzeichner course, that he could enrol in a Meisterschule (a school where he could train to become a master carpenter). He would be able to do two terms from the rehabilitation hospital and then the last term when he was at home. Shorsh was delighted: now at last his dream was coming true. He had to submit proof of his Aryan ancestry right back to his great grandfather on our father's side, not his great grandmother's, but as Shorsh looked like a real Aryan, tall, blond and blue eyed, the same as Toni, he had no problem and was invited to enrol. Only pure Aryans had permission to study. It was fortunate that no proof of Aryan ancestry was asked from our mother's side, that would not have been so easy, and I don't think even his blond hair and his blue eyes would have been of great help. Our mother had jet black hair and hazel eyes, my sister had chestnut coloured hair and hazel eyes. That proved that at some time in history another race must have come into our family. And while Shorsh researched our family history, he found that our great grandfather was a master carpenter in Allershausen, near Munich. Shorsh thought that could only be a good sign. But when it came to the actual enrolment, the professor told him that he could not possibly accept him, as he had a criminal record that said: Has attacked a superior officer. Shorsh was devastated and heavily disputed it. He said to the professor: "I have never attacked anybody in all my life, let alone a superior officer."

The professor felt very sorry for him and full of understanding said to him:

"You must have done something to warrant this accusation in your records. The date is end of February 1942. Go back and think about it. I am sure you will remember something, then came back to me and tell me what happened and I am quite sure we can resolve this problem."

Very depressed Shorsh went back and did exactly what the professor told him to do. He tried to remember and looked through the papers he had, and found nothing. What made it worse was that he knew that he would never attack anybody, let alone a superior officer. Yet he had the date when the alleged incident was supposed to have happened.

He had the date and he knew exactly where he had been. He had been in Engers, on the Mosel, in the war hospital called the Josefshaus. Then suddenly the memory hit him like a flash. Yes, if one considered the German's love for absolute accuracy, it could have possibly been construed as an attack on a superior officer.

When Shorsh was in Engers near Neuwied, on the Rhine in 1942, the soldiers had a fairly relaxed time. They could go out whenever they wanted, and they didn't have to report to anybody when they returned. At night the gate was closed at 8 o'clock, but the soldiers jumped over the wall and walked to their rooms. It was a well known habit of the wounded soldiers who could walk and neither the nurses nor the doctors objected.

It was on one of the days when Shorsh had been out with his girlfriend and returned to the hospital at 10 o'clock at night. As he was walking down the corridor to go to his room a young U.V.D. Unter Offizier vom Dienst (sergeant on duty) came towards him and demanded: "Where are you coming from?"

To which Shorsh answered quite innocently: "Oh, I just came in, I was out with my girl friend."

"Well," said the U.V.D. "You should have been here two hours ago!"

Shorsh thought that he noticed a slight irritation in the sergeant's voice, but dismissed the thought immediately, as nobody ever showed any interest in the time when the soldiers entered the hospital in the evening. So still quite nonplussed Shorsh answered: "Oh yes, but we don't keep to those hours, not those of us who can walk."

Shorsh's unconcerned answer really seemed to irritate this young U.V.D. He snapped at Shorsh:

"How dare you talk to me in this disrespectful manner? You should be standing to attention and saluting me."

This was just about the most ignorant remark any officer could have made. Shorsh couldn't have stood to attention to save his life. How he could possibly jump over the wall with his wounded leg and a walking stick was surprising. It couldn't have been a high wall. But now it was Shorsh's turn to get irritated. He changed his walking stick to his left hand and with his right hand he took him by the lapels and shook him a little, while asking:

"And exactly how do you expect me to do that? We have all just come back from the front and are pretty much messed up. What are you doing here, why aren't you on the front where you should be?"

But then he didn't feel that this officer was worth another thought, he left him standing there and just walked into his room and thought nothing more about it. Not so the officer, he reported Shorsh who received seven days imprisonment by sharp arrest. Sharp arrest meant imprisonment with only bread and water. Even in 1942 the prison warden wouldn't treat a heavily wounded soldier this way. The fact was, he had a terrific time in that prison. He had a proper bed, the door was never locked, his friends, his girlfriend, and girlfriends of friends could come and go as they pleased. He had no need of bread and water, as they brought him plenty of food and wine and magazines to read. They all had a ball. On the fifth day of his so-called imprisonment, he read in a magazine that it was against the law to imprison a seriously wounded soldier by sharp arrest. As the time was nearly up anyway and after all he had had a good time, he dismissed the whole affair and forgot all about it. Not for a moment did he think that he would have a criminal record. To him this incident was a trifle not worth thinking about and it went completely out of his head.

Shorsh then went straight back to the professor and told him the whole story. At first the professor started smiling, but quickly checked himself, and with a serious expression said:

"Well, you have been punished for your misdemeanour, so I don't see why we should continue."

Shorsh was immediately enrolled to attend the Meisterschule. For the first two terms he attended college from the hospital, then was discharged and the last term he attended from home. By then he could walk without a stick, but had to wear callipers up to his knee on his left foot for the rest of his life. In December 1944 he successfully finished college and was now a master carpenter, and was qualified to train apprentices. Our parents were delighted and for a time Shorsh worked as a master carpenter for a firm in Ismaning, which meant no travelling, much to the relief of our parents, as Munich was relentlessly bombarded.

My uncle, Hans Haberl, lived with his family in Munich, on Preising Strasse. He was the husband of my father's sister, Therese, and the father of Rosi, who used to visit Shorsh in hospital by dodging the porters. In 1944 the two sons were already married. Their older son Anton lived in Ismaning and their younger son Hans still lived in Munich, on Wörth Strasse.

On Sunday 17th December 1944, from 9 o'clock until 11 o'clock in the evening, in a terrific air-raid over Munich, one huge bomb demolished five houses at the crossroads of Stein and Preising Strasse. Hans, the younger son, who lived not far from the devastation, was the first on the scene. He found it difficult to believe what he saw. He knew that he had at once to organise a rescue. His wife, Katharina, went on her bicycle to Ismaning to alert Anton who in turn went to my parents' house to ask Shorsh to help in the rescue. A local butcher, Kunz by name, lent them his car and with shovel and pickaxe they went to rescue the people in the cellars. They really did think that people had survived in the cellars. The two sons, Hans and Anton, knew exactly where their parents and sister had been sitting and thought they would have no problem locating them. Uncle Hans on one occasion had taken Shorsh to show him the cellar he had fortified with tree

trunks and said: "Look at that, nothing can get through here."
Shorsh was amazed and had to agree with him.

So, full of confidence they started digging, but after two
days trying to build a shaft into the cellar they had to accept
that they needed more people and heavier equipment. Then a
builder known to the two sons started to help them. To their
delight they made good progress and on the third day the
shaft reached the cellar. When the opening into the cellar was
still small Anton called through: "Father! Mother! Rosi!"

But all that came back was the echo. When eventually
they reached them all, the occupants were dead. The tree
trunks, uncle Hans was so proud of, had all fallen over,
probably just before an enormous bomb struck the houses.
The pressure wave must have collapsed the tree trunks thus
giving no support to the cellar.

On the third day, when Shorsh came home, the first
thing my parents asked was: "Are they all right?"

There was an eerie atmosphere in the house. I had a cup
of coffee in my hand, not real coffee but coffee substitute. I
felt very uncomfortable, and while Shorsh went to sit down it
all seemed an eternity. It can't have taken more than a
minute, if that. It was all so unreal and in my child's logic I
tried to get some reality into the situation and asked Shorsh:
"Would you like a sip of my coffee?"

He turned his head towards me and smiled, a smile that
I couldn't forget if I lived to a thousand years. It was the
saddest smile I had ever seen in my life, before or after. Then
quietly and calmly he said:

"They are all dead. All of them, in all the five houses.
They didn't stand a chance."

With that he put his head into his right hand, bent
forward and supported it with his elbow on his knee, and
cried bitterly. That young man, who had taken part in the
Russian campaign in the east and had looked death in the eye
many times, just broke down and cried bitterly. He came
home under the illusion that home was not a war zone, and
had to come to terms with the fact that war had followed him
home.

After a little while he managed to say:

"All the bodies have been taken to a nearby protestant church. There were 32 of them."

When the bodies were recovered, the body of uncle Hans was not with his wife Therese and his daughter Rosi. Uncle Hans was an air-raid warden and during air-raids he had to go through the five cellars to make sure everybody was accounted for. He was on his rounds when the bomb struck, therefore he was not sitting with his wife and daughter. But because of that, the authorities decided that he had to be buried in a mass grave with all the other bodies and not with his family. However the two sons fought hard to get the body of their father released in order that he could be buried together with his family on 23rd December 1944.

Chapter Twenty Four

WW2 in Finland.
Joke about Goering.
Jagdkompanie (Hunting Company) goes on reconnaissance.
Winter starts early.
Hospital ship, Monte Rosa.
Toni and Sepp are separated. Sepp is transferred to a hospital in Oslo, Norway. Toni is transferred to Trondheim.

Although my parents were delighted that their eldest son was at home and received an honourable discharge on 19th January 1944 due to his injuries, they were still desperately worried about their younger son Toni. His letters arrived very infrequently and did not say a lot. In 1944 it didn't need a militarist to see where the war was going. On 23rd June 1944, General Dietl visited once more the mountaineers with two friends. While flying back to Berlin the aircraft exploded over Rettenegg, a small village in Finland.

In spite of all the atrocities committed by the Nazis, there were still some who dared make sarcastic jokes about them. Father once came home with a joke he had heard at work. Göring was generally known as the pig.

The joke went like this: One day during the war Mrs. Goering bought a piglet on the black market. To take it home she dressed it up as a baby and put it into a pram. On the way home a neighbour met her and congratulated her on her baby. She looked into the pram and exclaimed: Oh, what a lovely baby, he looks exactly like his father!

People in Ismaning seemed to enjoy this joke immensely.

On 3rd September 1944, until 29th November, the Mountaineers went from North Finland to Narvik and were heavily engaged in defence.

On 4th October 1944 both Toni and Sepp, our cousin, had to take part in reconnaissance, as both belonged to the Jagdkompanie, unit 139. From every battalion one company had to take part in reconnaissance to find out where the Russian army was situated. To have knowledge of the whereabouts of the Russian troops was vitally important for the German troops to be able to secure their retreat, because by now that was all they could do. Reaching Murmansk had by now become a dream. The Mountaineers had to find a way to look for the Russian troops without being seen.

Winter had already started. On the first day of reconnaissance it was raining and they had to get through marshes in the Karelian jungle, then at the end of the first day it started snowing incessantly. The temperature plummeted to 25 and 30 degrees below Zero. It took them three days to estimate the location of the Russian troops. The whole reconnaissance troop, 71 men, at first had to cope with relentless rain and then with snow in subzero temperatures, inadequately clothed, and without shelter whatsoever, except the trees, which they could not cut in case of being discovered. All they could do was huddle together in the snow. When they did get back to their troops they were suffering severely from frostbite on their feet, hands, face and ears. The frostbite of a few Mountaineers proved to be too severe to receive first aid. A sergeant took the soldiers with the most severe frostbite to a small village near Kautokeino, in the Karelian jungle, as a doctor visited there on a sleigh pulled by reindeer. As soon as Toni and Sepp arrived there with the rest of the Mountaineers from the reconnaissance, they wanted to go back to their company, thinking that their feet were not frostbitten as they did not feel anything. The Doctor did not permit that, but told them to take off their ski boots, which to their surprise was not an easy task, but needed the help of the paramedics. The socks had become part of their feet as through the frost, socks and feet had become one, and the paramedics could only take them off after dowsing their feet with cold water, and once the socks had been taken off the paramedics rubbed their feet with snow. They suffered excruciating pain. Both had second to third degree frostbite. Both Toni and Sepp developed on either side of each foot a large blister. Then all the Mountaineers with frostbite were taken farther back from the front on an Akkiar, which looked like a boat and was pulled by reindeer. It took one day until they were put up in a Schwedentempel (Swedish Temple). Here there were more medical staff and all the soldiers received tetanus injections. The next day came a bus from Kowdor, which ran on wood gas, to take them to Alakurtti, but between Kowdor and Alakurtti they were snowed in for two days until a snow blower came to clear the way. Once the way was clear, the bus was able to take all the soldiers to Kautokeino. Here, some very inventive paramedics transformed a horse stable into a makeshift hospital, which accommodated only soldiers who had frostbite on their feet. The colonel doctor looked at all the soldiers' feet and those with the worst frostbite had to be transferred to the hospital ship Monte Rosa that was docked on the coast. In peace time it was a K.D.F. Ship (Kraft durch Freude - strength through joy). Workers could go on holiday on it. Now it was used to transport sick and wounded soldiers. It had no armoury.

From Kautokeino all the sick soldiers were transported by military ambulances to the coast, and on wooden stretchers crane-lifted onto the Monte Rosa. The medical staff transformed the dining rooms into sick bays, and for the first time the sick and wounded soldiers received proper medical care. The ship moved slowly and often stopped altogether. Toni and Sepp's blisters had to be taken off, as well as their toenails, this was done without anaesthetic. After two days on the ship, Toni developed an abscess on his tonsils, and while he was waiting for his treatment he had to witness a foot amputation, which he thought was the worst thing he had ever seen. His abscess was lanced, without anaesthetic, which was not altogether bad, as soon as it was over the pain had gone. The feet of some of the soldiers started to get black and sadly had to be amputated. But the rest of the soldiers had their feet put into iron cages, this was to give the feet a chance do dry. Yet going to the toilet proved to be a problem. Those young men did not want to use either a bottle or a bedpan, so they crawled to the toilet and from every bed a trail of blood indicated the way to the toilet.

Toni and Sepp had problems with their feet for the rest of their lives. Sometimes they suffered from unbearable itching, so much so that they rubbed them with rough towels until they started bleeding, but in the winter the skin broke and left them with a soreness equally terrible.

At the beginning of March 1945, Toni was transferred to Trondheim in Norway and it was here where Toni and

Sepp, for the first time in the war, had to separate. Toni's feet developed a very thin skin, so thin that he could not bear to wear socks against his feet; instead he rapped them in soft flannel cloths and pulled his socks over them.

Sepp was transferred to Oslo, to a military hospital as his feet by then had not healed. Toni was ordered to the front in Trondheim, but as he arrived there the officers asked for volunteers to go back 50 km to Störn. Toni and two of his friends volunteered with two other soldiers, they thought and hoped, just a few kilometres nearer home.

Camp in Narvik

Above: Captain Fritz Reinmüller
Below: Captain Fritz Reinmüller on the Eismeerstrasse

Toni's bunker in Narvik

Toni leaning against his bunker

Chapter Twenty Five

Toni and his friends refuse to be separated.
The three friends are billeted in the same barrack
- 12 soldiers in one barrack.
The soldiers had to guard the Hagerbruecke Bridge.

The three friends were my brother, Toni Huber, Walter Gerstgrasser, and Karl Langhans. The commanding officer was sergeant-major Dr. Freund. The sergeant-major tried to separate the three friends, but they refused to be separated, so he gave in and all three friends were billeted in the same barrack that accommodated 12 soldiers. In Störn they had to guard a bridge the Germans called Hagerbruecke. All the soldiers had two hours guard duty each on the bridge, day and night. It was difficult for them to keep strictly to the schedule, as they liked going out. So they covered for each other, but always made it up so that none of the soldiers lost out.

Sergeant-major Dr. Freund, who was a journalist and had already served in the First World War, was very kind to the young soldiers and didn't restrict their little escapades, as long as there was always someone guarding the bridge.

On the night of 7th to 8th May 1945, Toni was on guard duty in the morning a 3 o'clock. He had made friends with Peter who was a native of Norway and worked at the railway. He gave Toni the key to the railway hut so that the three friends could make a fire at night. On this particular night Toni lit a fire before going on guard duty on the bridge. The bridge was on a hill, and by now the soldiers didn't take their duty very seriously any more, they knew it was all over. He fell asleep in the railway hut and his friends did not wake him. Dr. Freund was off duty on this day and had left, but had appointed Walter, Toni's friend, as his deputy.

Suddenly they heard two shots. Toni woke up, ran out of the hut and up towards the bridge, on the way he met two soldiers and thinking that it was they who had fired the shots, he shouted at them:

"What's the matter with you, are you crazy?"

They told him that they were accompanying the O.v.O (Offizier vom Ortsdienst - officer of the local troops) who was on the bridge and had fired the shots because there was nobody on guard.

"We are his driver and his escort."

Toni quite naturally thought that he could bluff his way out of a hazardous situation, and said to the soldiers:

"Don't worry; don't say anything, I'll talk to the officer."

He ran up the hill to the O.v.O, saluted very respectfully and explained that he had heard something under the bridge and had gone to investigate. The officer was satisfied and drove off with his two companions. But Toni counted on the discretion of the two soldiers, who in fact betrayed him. And at 5 o'clock the officer came back with his companions. By then Toni was back in his barrack. The officer sounded the wake-up alarm. Walter came out of the barrack and asked the officer:

"What do you want me to do? I can't wake everybody up just because there was no guard on the bridge for a few minutes."

The officer was furious and shouted:

"I am not going to have a l4 - 18!"

He was referring to the First World War, which he knew Dr. Freund had served in. It was quite obvious that he did not think too much of Dr. Freund and his discipline, or was there some jealousy involved as Dr Freund was so highly respected by all the soldiers. It could also have been that he thought that WW2 should not end as WW1 had ended - in capitulation by the Germans. The soldiers didn't exactly know what he meant by his reference to 14 - 18. Again he shouted: "Sound the alarm and tell everybody to fall in!"

Walter had no choice but to do as he was told. As soon as everybody had fallen in, the officer said:

"Der Alarm ist beendet." ("The alarm is finished.")

Walter was very angry at that, as he saw no sense in it at all. He told the troops that they could all go back into the barracks, turned to go back to his barrack dragging his rifle on the floor, holding it by the barrel. When the officer saw that, he shouted:

"Soldier, is your rifle loaded?"

"Of course it's loaded."

Came Walter's answer. And still holding it by the barrel he picked it up and threw it into his barrack where it landed with an almighty crash. The officer threatened Walter with his pistol and shouted:

"No 14 -18!"

And followed him with his companions into the barrack, shouting:

"You are all going to be court-martialled for your insubordination!"

Toni, trying to calm the situation, only managed to make it worse when he said:

"Jetzt hörst Du aber auf, steck Deinen Kopf in einen Eiskübel und kühl Dich ab." ("Give over, put your head in a bucket of ice and cool down.")

What made matters worse was that Toni spoke to him in Bavarian instead of High German as he was supposed to, and he also addressed him with the familiar Du and not the formal Sie, which was another offence. So he too was threatened with court-martial. Then the three friends threw the officer with his companions out of the barrack. There they could do nothing but drive off. But at 8 o'clock the military police came to pick up Toni and Walter. It was fortunate for them that the police did not take them away from the camp but took them to an empty barrack for interrogation. Now the two mountaineers started to become incredibly worried, even at this late stage in the war, the situation looked dire for them and they knew it. But to their great relief the interrogation had hardly begun when Dr. Freund, the sergeant major, entered the room and said:

"Meine Herren Deutschland hat kapituliert, es ist jetzt bedingungslos was mit uns passiert." ("Gentlemen, Germany has capitulated, and it doesn't really matter what happens to us now.")

Which meant there would be no court-martial. Toni and Walter stood up and saluted with great respect. Only when they arrived back at their barrack could they air their incredible relief and happiness. The whole barrack was filled with laughter, congratulating each other. At last all they were waiting for had eventually come. The war was over and they could all go home. They actually believed that, they were convinced that within a few weeks they would be all at home.

The Mountaineers at
their outpost in Störn

Chapter Twenty Six

Bombers droning over Munich. 8 bombs fall on one farm.
Shorsh built an air raid shelter in the forest.
A low-flying plane.
An elderly gentleman boards the wrong train.
Air-raids increase at an alarming rate.
Civilian prisoners from Russia and Ukraine.

Bombing had already started in 1942, and got steadily worse. As there was no industry in Ismaning to speak of, people thought themselves relatively safe, there was no reason why it should be bombed. At that time, the only industry was the sauerkraut factory and the brick factory about 3 km to the south, on the main road to Munich. Gradually the bombing increased. Then tragically during one bombing raid, eight bombs fell on one farm, mainly on the stables. A maid and a French prisoner, who was assigned to work on the farm, were killed while working in the stable.

Shorsh had built an air raid shelter in the side of a hill, in the nearby forest, and so had many other men.

The bombing raids still came mainly at night. Sometimes we had a night without a bombing raid, which was wonderful and when I woke up in the morning, I could hardly believe that I had slept all night and in amazement would ask my mother:

"Weren't there any bombing raids last night?"

She used to laugh and ask in return: "Do you miss them?"

"Oh, no." Would come my answer. "It's lovely to sleep all night."

Those lovely nights became rarer very quickly. The nearer the front came to Germany, the more frequently came the air raids. Once, in 1943, when I was on my way home from school, a lone aeroplane came droning along. Suddenly it fell into a dive and flying low, fired one of it's machine guns down the street. Somehow nobody in the street was hurt, but in the train station was a stationary train with only one elderly man sitting in it and he was shot through the window right into his heart, still sitting there but dead. Later it was discovered that he got onto the wrong train on the Ostbahnhof

(East Station in Munich). He had stayed on the train to go back to Munich and change to the right train. In the evening I told Shorsh the aeroplane had made a peculiar noise. It did not sound like shots being fired, it sounded something like 'Tachue, tachue'. Shorsh then explained to me what I had heard so distinctly were ricochets, and then I received the full expert explanation of what ricochets were.

Sometimes there were 2 air raids in one night. It was terribly hard to get up and dress quickly, mother would dress Emil, my little nephew, Anni dressed her children, both women each had a handbag ready, containing important papers and of course those all important and precious ration cards. Then we ran to the forest into the air-raid shelter. The street would be filled with people running, a multitude of people. As well as the people from Ismaning there were also people who had been bombed in Munich and now lived in emergency accommodation in our village, and all were running towards air-raid shelters. To me it seemed as if the whole world was on the move. Then it meant sitting in a damp air raid shelter, cold and miserable and often not completely dressed. I usually wore only one stocking as I was never quick enough to put both my stockings on. Wearing shoes, normally one or two sizes too large, I sat in the shelter with my legs pulled up hugging them to my body for warmth and trying to cover them with my coat, which was also too big. At least I had no difficulties in covering my legs with it. For clothes and shoes we needed coupons from the council, which were almost impossible to obtain. I received one pair of short boots during the war years. Otherwise it was clothes from adults made smaller, but if we wore them too big, we didn't grow out of them.

When the all-clear sounded we all came out of the shelters, like rabbits coming out of their warrens, cold and weary we trudged up the hill. Once when we reached our house and looked towards Munich we saw the sky alight. Munich was burning! The people who lost their homes in bombing raids usually found their way into the country; it was in Ismaning or other surrounding villages where they could find somewhere to live, even if it was only a spare room in somebody's house. It was even more tragic when civilian prisoners, mainly from Russia or the Ukraine, were sometimes able to leave their camp in Munich-Freimann, and they came to us begging for a piece of bread or some thread. It was heartbreaking. They were mainly women and children.

The bombing raids came relentlessly. The nearer the front came to Germany the more often came the bombing raids. Food became ever shorter. And mother still managed to send biscuits to Toni in Finland. Sending parcels to the front became very much restricted. The authorities restricted food parcels to the front to 50 grams (This is not a mistake, it actually was 50 grams). Yet the authorities did not count on the inventiveness of my mother. She still had a hand-operated sewing machine. She used brown paper, folded it into a little squares and sewed it closed on three sides, making a little envelope, then pushed a biscuit into the little paper envelope and sewed it closed. But did not cut the thread, instead folded the next little envelope, sewed it again on three sides pushed a biscuit into the little pocket and sewed it closed. Now there were two little brown paper envelopes with one biscuit in each, still attached one to the other. Thus she carried on until she had a string of 15 little brown envelopes with one biscuit in each. Yet each of them not exceeding the authorised 50 grams. Toni received every string of biscuits. The soldiers who delivered the post did not even bother to look at the address, as they all knew whenever a string of little brown paper envelopes arrived, it was Toni's. They would simply hold it up and call Toni's name. He also received all my letters. There must have been a great many, as to this day I remember his postal code, 18 3 94 D.

Chapter Twenty Seven

Desperate food shortage. Mother exchanges sugar for flour.
French prisoners of war in the gym hall.
Mother is happy to help farmers.
Food becomes ever more scarce. Mother is paid with sugar beet.
The sugar beet syrup.
December 1944, the lost Christmas spirit.

As 1944 approached, food became ever shorter, as the front came ever nearer to Germany. For us this meant that air-raids increased at a frightening rate. Not only did we have to get up at night, now they started in the daytime as well. Food became evermore scarce. People would give anything for bread or anything else that could be eaten. Women used to give their wedding rings in exchange for bread. My mother usually gave one pound of sugar to the local miller whenever she was desperately short of flour, as he would give her 10 pounds of flour for every pound of sugar she gave him. Sugar was very rare indeed. Every child received one pound of sugar per month on the ration cards. Adults received only half a pound. On birthdays we usually got a spoon of sugar in our coffee (coffee substitute). As my parents cared for two children, my nephew Emil and myself, they were allowed 2 pounds of sugar for us on the ration cards. One pound often went to the miller; the rest had to do for everything else where sugar was needed. Yes, the miller always gave my mother 10 pounds of flour for every pound of sugar she brought to him, but he did not do it out of the goodness of his heart, sugar was just so valuable. Then it happened that mother went to see him without sugar one day. She just hadn't any left, but she needed flour desperately. I was with her on that day. I am sure she took me along hoping the miller would feel kindly towards her when he saw her with a thin little girl. But not so! Quite sternly he told her he did not have any. Mother knew that this was not so. She knew very well, if she had brought a pound of sugar, he wouldn't have been short of flour. She tried to change his mind, telling him that she had to send some biscuits to Toni in Finland and that the war wouldn't last forever and she would come to buy flour from him when we could buy everything again. I wanted to leave and started tugging on her sleeve. But she wouldn't go and was really begging.

"Please," she kept saying. Give me just a little flour that I can go home and cook something."

He became more and more annoyed with her, and in the end just to get rid of her he put a little flour into a linen sack and threw it in front of her feet, on the floor. Mother bent down and picked it up and thanked him profusely. The following month she brought him a pound of sugar again and he was not short of flour. He was not the kind of man, or the kind of human being even, who would have had any idea to what humiliation he subjected my mother. Now writing this I am thinking, wouldn't it have been wonderful if my mother could have taken the small sack of flour and thrown it back at him? But she was a mother and would have endured any humiliation to be able to feed her children.

Although in 1944 one didn't have to be a genius to know that however keen the Nazis still were, the war was going the wrong way for them. Newsflashes on the radio had ceased completely and however much the propaganda minister, Dr. Göbbels was shouting, not many people believed him, if any. Yet the Nazis were now more dangerous then ever. In the park, which was called Hain, in the middle of Ismaning, was the local gym hall, except in 1944 it was used for another recreation, if one could call it that, it housed French prisoners of war. Very often they had permission to go for exercise past our house, into the forest to the river Isar, accompanied by the warden. On one of those days mother was sweeping the yard, with me helping her, when the French prisoners walked by. The warden stopped at the fence to talk to my mother. To her horror he said: "Just look at them, I could shoot the lot."

Mother took my hand and quickly went into the house. She was visibly shaking.

When in the evening she told Father, he asked: "Did they come back?"

"Oh, yes." Mother said. "I was watching, I don't think he would have dared to do anything."

Father answered:

"You mean shoot them, no, I don't think he would have dared, he just enjoyed having a big mouth and frightening you, they have to have their sadistic pleasures."

Mother still helped the farmers and was only too glad when she was asked, as it meant extra food. Very often in early autumn she and a friend would start clearing a field of sugar beet. The two women pulled them out and cut off the leaves, threw them on a heap and I walked behind them picking up the leaves to cover every small heap of sugar beet with, to stop them from drying out before the farmer came to load them onto the cart. In payment for this work they would receive some of the sugar beet. It was a job women liked doing, as it was thought good payment. The sugar beet was diced and boiled until very soft, then strained through a cloth and pressed out, the juice was then boiled again until it became brown syrup. We children thought it was wonderful. We used it as jam on bread, it was lovely and sweet. And when mother happened not to look in our direction we quickly took a teaspoonful out of the jar.

I remember an occasion later, in 1948, when it was easy to buy food again, that Emil and I remembered that lovely sugar beet syrup. We asked mother to cook us some of that lovely syrup again. Mother refused point blank to do so and said: "I am not cooking that rubbish again, when we can make jam."

"Oh, no!" We exclaimed. "It was lovely, we always liked it."

"Of course you liked it." Came her answer. "You liked everything you got between your teeth. But believe me it was not lovely, but it was food, and nutritious."

But we kept nagging her to make some of that lovely syrup again. At last, just to have her peace again, she went to the trouble of making a small jar. What a delight it was to see it on the breakfast table! I was the first to try, then I pushed it to Emil. He whispered to me: "I don't like it."

"No, I don't either." I whispered back.

It was really not very nice, to say the least. Then I hid the jar in the bread bin behind the bread. It didn't take long until mother found it and was very cross.

"I told you that you wouldn't like it, but no, you had to have it. I really should make you eat it now, after you were nagging me for days."

But her anger did not last and we didn't have to eat it. Father of course laughed when she told him. But all this happened after the war.

For now war was still raging and bombs were still falling. Air-raids, so far nocturnal occurrences, had now become a regular daytime horror. In December 1944 Christmas spirit was something that had happened in the past. People would say: "When we had Christmas....." And then they would recite what they would cook and eat. Food was always the first thing they would speak about. Then came the Christmas tree. Well, where could you get one? You certainly couldn't buy one. With the whole village in darkness, and no Midnight Mass, what was there to celebrate? The only light we could sometimes see was the full moon and that frightened the life out of everybody, because of the snow on the ground and the light of the full moon, nights sometimes became as bright as daylight so that the bombers had it easy. Towards the end of 1944, the front advanced rapidly against Germany. Therefore when the air-raid warning siren went off we had barely enough time to dress before the bombers would be heard droning overhead. What frightened us children most was that dreadful noise. The antiaircraft gun was hammering away, the bombers droning overhead and the searchlights trying to spot them. Always two long beams reaching right up into the sky crossing each other and trying their utmost to get a bomber into the crossbeam so that the antiaircraft gun could shoot it down. I don't think that they were overly successful. All that and the streets filled with people running, infants crying, only to end up in a cold and damp air-raid shelter. It was bedlam day after day and night after night. Some Christmas! To be without a Christmas tree in Bavaria is just unthinkable. So on 24th of December 1944 when it was dusk, Shorsh put on his coat and mother asked him: "Where are you going?"

"I'll be back soon." Came the answer. Mother knew at once what he had in mind and wasn't too keen on the idea, and told him so.

"If you are caught, you'll be in a concentration camp, and even your wounded leg won't help you."

But he tried to allay her fear when he said: "Just look out there, it is pitch black in the forest, who could see me there?"

Father was outside locking up the outhouse and the chicken coup. I too, of course knew what Shorsh was up to. I thought it was wonderful; he was going to fetch a Christmas tree! I was so excited and of course wanted to be in on it, but knew very well that I would never get permission to go with him. Sometimes a child can become invisible. Mother was busy worrying about Shorsh and didn't notice me slipping out of the kitchen, opening the door to the cellar where just inside on the wall, father's gardening jacket was hanging on a nail sticking out of the wall. A pair of mother's old shoes was always at the top of the stairs, they had no shoelaces but strings, which did the job of tying up the shoes. Quickly, I put on father's gardening jacket and slipped on mother's old shoes, tied them up and the fact that they didn't fit was of no great consequence to me, I was used to shoes at least one size to big for me. Father's gardening jacket came down to my ankles, which was just as well as it was cold and frosty outside, and the sleeves covered my hands completely, so I didn't need any gloves. Dressed like this I slipped out of the house unnoticed, I tried to catch up with my brother, but didn't quite manage it. Once he entered the forest he was swallowed up by the darkness. By the time I reached the forest I saw no sign of him and I too was enveloped by the darkness. All I saw was blackness around me, and that terrified me, so I let out an almighty scream which brought Shorsh back in no time. He scowled at me and in a low voice: "What are you doing here?"

Quite innocently I answered in the same low voice: "I want to come with you."

Shorsh was so angry when he realised that he was now lumbered with me, he hissed at me: "If you don't keep up with me, I'll leave you here and never come back for you."

And I believed him, because this is exactly how older brothers talk. I did keep up with him, just. He was walking and I was running. He knew exactly where he was going, he must have been there before. Yet at the time it didn't dawn on me. Only much later I asked him and he admitted.

"Oh, yes, I had chosen that tree some time before."

It was a beautiful tree, just the right size for our kitchen-cum-sitting room. It was standing in a little clearing. Shorsh had a small saw tucked under his jacket and started sawing it down. I just sank to the ground. I was so exhausted. But now seeing this lovely tree, I was glad that I had come. I said: "Oh, it's lovely."

Shorsh turned and very gently asked: "Do you like it? Do you think it will look nice when we have decorated it?"

"Oh, yes." I said. "It will look beautiful."

All his anger had gone and on the way home he took care that I could keep up with him. Everything went well until we came home.

When Father came in from locking up the outhouses, Mother of course told him where Shorsh had gone. He was furious, and when we came in with the Christmas tree he flew at Shorsh shouting about what a stupid thing he had done. Didn't he realise how dangerous this could have been for him and the whole family? Especially where he himself was not exactly popular. That sort of thing would give the Nazis a wonderful excuse to get him. I had never seen my father so angry. Suddenly he noticed me and bellowed: "And where did you come from? Just look at you, you look like a tramp!"

They had not even noticed that I had been gone as well. Very gingerly I said: "I went with Shorsh." And to help Shorsh I said: "I followed him."

That didn't make it any easier, father took no notice of that and continued shouting: "Now he is turning his sister into a thief!"

I didn't understand the meaning of this, because to my way of thinking we had not stolen anything. Stealing to me was taking something from another person, which we did not do. Taking a Christmas tree from our forest was not steeling. That tree did not belong to anybody. It was one of those things again which I did not understand and again I did not ask. I thought father was angry enough. But we did have a lovely Christmas tree, and no air-raid. The tree was beautifully decorated. We still had Christmas decorations from since before the war. I thought they looked beautiful, although some of the baubles were broken, but mother turned them so that only the good side was visible.

Chapter Twenty Eight

Air-raids continue. Where is the front?
Father and Shorsh have discussions with friends.
There hasn't been a letter from Toni for a long time.
The number of birch crosses continues to increase.

Although there were no air-raids over Christmas, we didn't
have to wait very long. Where was the front? Sometimes a
friend of father's would come in the evening to discuss the
war with him and Shorsh. I used to sit on the corner bench in
the kitchen being absolutely fascinated with all that was
going on. Nobody took any notice of me. As I have
mentioned before, a quiet child can become quite invisible,
and nothing was more fascinating for me than to listen in to
adults talking. Shorsh thought that the front must be very near
as the air-raids came so frequently. It was obvious to him that
they didn't have to come very far. On the news very little was
said about the front. People in general thought it was going
towards the end. Toni hadn't written for some time. But then
just after New Year 1945, came a letter from him just saying
it was very cold, but he was well. It was a very short letter,
my parents wondered why. Was it too dangerous for him to
write where he was? What was going on? The little birch
crosses in our cemetery were still increasing at an alarming
rate. That showed that soldiers were still dying and people
were wondering why. As the opinion of most men was that it
couldn't go on much longer. Of course opinions could only
be uttered behind closed doors.

March 1945, the snow was melting and and despite war,
spring could not be stopped from coming. Spring flowers
started to bloom in the forest regardless of what was going on
in the world, and we children used to pick them to take home
to our mothers. I tried to cheer my mother up with little
bunches of violets; she really did need cheering up. She was
so happy to receive little bunches of violets or cowslips. I
knew that she cried a lot. Toni's letters hadn't come for some
time now. Father and Shorsh tried to comfort her by saying
that it was not surprising, the post must be in an awful mess.
Even if he wrote a dozen letters, they probably would never
get through. She tried so hard to still create a normal family

life. Summer was on its way and farmers would ask for her help again.

One afternoon she came home with a lump of butter. It must have been at least half a pound. She had baked a few rolls the day before and was delighted to show me the butter. Butter was something we rarely saw. She said to me: "Come here my girl, I'll give you something really good to eat."

She cut a roll in half and spread it thickly with butter. I thought I had never tasted anything so nice in all my life. When I took a bite and swished the butter around in my mouth it tasted like nothing I had eaten before. I couldn't believe anything could taste that nice. Mother enjoyed watching me eating it. But alas! I hadn't even finished the buttered roll, when it all came up again. It was too rich for my stomach. Mother was so disappointed.

"For once I give her something good to eat, then she goes and vomits it all up again."

She was so downhearted about it. She was sad that it hadn't worked out the way she thought. Then she thought of something else which she knew would make me happy. She went to the cupboard, took the jar of sugar beet syrup, gave me a dessert spoon and said: "Here you are, you can take a whole spoonful of syrup, you'd like that wouldn't you?"

Didn't I just, and I could keep that down, no problem. That made me forget the butter very quickly.

Chapter Twenty Nine

Mother's yearly pilgrimage. Shorsh goes to college by train.
Father goes to work and sees Shorsh catching the moving train.
Father comes home in a paralytic state.
Ismaning and euthanasia.

Every year at Whitsuntide mother went on a pilgrimage to
Altötting, a well known shrine of Our Lady, in Bavaria. This
pilgrimage is a yearly occurrence at every Whitsuntide.
About thirty or forty inhabitants of Ismaning go on this
pilgrimage, and by go I mean they walk the 50 km or so.
They walk it in two days and the same on the way back.
Mother went on this pilgrimage every year and not even the
war could stop her. She would say: "I know the mother of
God will bring my sons home."

But when Toni's letters stopped coming she must have
had her doubts, because her tears flowed so easily.

Father and Shorsh went to Munich every morning on
the 05:45 train: Father to work at the E.V.M. and Shorsh to
college. Shorsh was studying to become an engineer in Hoch
und Tiefbau (high and low building). In Bavaria you have
high building, that is everything that is built above the road
and low building, that is everything below the road, such as
drainage. Every morning father woke Shorsh at 5 o'clock to
get ready to catch the train. He himself started off at 5.30 am
to go to the train station to catch his train, he was never late.
Friends usually occupied the same wagon. The wooden
benches on the train didn't provide a lot of comfort, but then
the journey only took 30 minutes. Father spent the journey
with his friends, usually deep in conversation or reading the
newspaper, always the Fölkischer Beobachter (People's
Observer) the only newspaper in Nazi Germany.

Shorsh was always late as he found it too hard to get up
that early in the morning. Then one morning one of father's
friends, pointing to the window, said: "Shorsh," (my father's
name was also Shorsh.) "Look out there."

Father was horrified when he saw his son jumping over
the barrier and onto the moving train. His friend told him that
this would happen every morning. Shorsh didn't need a
ticket, as he was a wounded soldier, transport was free for

him. Normally passengers had to walk through a gate in the barrier and show the official attending the gate their ticket. But as Shorsh did not need a ticket he just jumped the barrier, because the gate was closed and the train had started moving. From that day on Shorsh was never late again catching the train. Father woke him and stayed with him until he was out of bed. Father didn't even bother to tell him off, he just said: "I have seen you jumping on the moving train."

It was also at about the same time when father still worked at the E.V.M., the soup kitchen, when the workers came across a small barrel of schnapps. They had no idea where it came from. It was hidden behind some boxes. They had no idea who the person was who had hidden it. Perhaps somebody hid it in a hurry and had no opportunity to pick it up? This person might even have been killed in an air-raid. What could they possibly do? One thing that came to minds - they could drink it. They could have given it up to the authorities (the Nazis), but nobody thought of that, at least nobody suggested it. So on general agreement it was decided that they would drink it. They thought Christmas had come again. They knocked a hole in the top, pushed a rubber tube into it and emptied the whole barrel of Schnapps. Eight people, men and women, drank the barrel of schnapps. It was a small barrel, but too much for eight people. Especially when alcoholic drinks were completely unobtainable. It was still possible to get a kind of beer with. I say a kind of beer, because it was very thin and the alcohol content was very low. One certainly could not get drunk on it. Those women and men hadn't had schnapps for years, or any other alcoholic drink. Suddenly they were drinking it using a tube pushed into a barrel. They must all have been paralytic, because I remember my father coming home in this state. He never remembered how he managed to get to the station at the Ostbahnhof and how he got on the train. A young man, who knew father well, Erhard Schmidramsl was his name, looked after him on the train. When eventually the train arrived in Ismaning, Erhard went to the bicycle repair shop Rösch, quite near the station and borrowed a wheelbarrow. With that he went back to the station and with the help of the stationmaster put father into the wheelbarrow and wheeled him home. A friend of Erhard's came with him. On arriving, the two young men more or less dragged him out of the wheelbarrow, into the house and put him on the concrete floor in the hall. When I saw that, I started to cry, I thought father had had an accident, or else he was very ill. Erhard quickly tried to allay my fears, he said: "You don't need to cry girl, he is only drunk." To mother he said: "Leave him lying here until he comes round."

My little nephew Emil, who was then 4 years old, sat down by his shoulder, and stayed there until father started to move. He, too, was very concerned about his grandfather. When eventually he started to move and moan, Mother dragged him outside into the yard and threw him into an old chair. It took all her strength. He had his legs apart and started retching. He would have fallen off the chair, but mother held him back by his shoulders, standing behind him. And then it started. I had never seen anything like that and never since. He started to vomit, but he did not vomit as people do when they are unwell. He opened his mouth and liquid came out as if from a fountain. It looked exactly like that, and it came and it came. I was so astonished and asked Mother: "How much more?"

She shrugged her shoulders. She had never seen anything like this either. After what seemed a long time, it gradually stopped. Again just like a fountain, at first the liquid came less and less and then a trickle before it stopped altogether.

The next day he told us what had happened. He took such pleasure in telling us how the women laughed and how they danced around. As he was telling us we too had to laugh. It was something so rare to see women laugh in those days. We, too, took delight in it when he told us, there was so little to laugh about. But we were still the fortunate ones, in comparison with the people in concentration camps. The Nazis tried to make sure that we didn't hear all that was going on in those camps, but the things we did hear were blood curdling. Untermenschen (Subhumans) was the name the Nazis gave to the Jews and people from the conquered eastern countries, who were transported to Germany into labour camps.

This farming community, on which the war effort depended, was not exempt from these utterly inhuman activities. In Ismaning lived several families with mentally handicapped family members. As it was, their life was extremely hard without the Nazis. Education was practically unheard of for these people. Special schools or teachers did not exist. On the whole these children were just left on the back bench in mainstream schools. Once they had reached school leaving age, they stayed with their family and performed very simple work, and they often had to endure the mockery of the people who lived in the same community. Very often they were used as scapegoats should a barn burn in the village. If the burden for the families became too much they could apply for a place in a care home. But while the families believed that their sons and daughters would live in a safe and comfortable environment, the Nazis saw them as humans not worthy of living. They were regarded a burden for the community on the whole, and a disastrous racial doctrine gave them the reason for the belief that this barbarity was right. This annihilation of the so called worthless humans started on the 1st September 1939, on the day war started. On this day Hitler gave the order for the mass killing of handicapped and sick people. For 2 years, following this specific order, 70 to 80.000 patients were legally killed in Germany's nursing and care homes.

Also Ismaning did not escape from this barbarity. At the start of the war the affected families received in short intervals, one after the other, the same news: their son or daughter had unfortunately died of pneumonia or unexplainable circumstances, and the body would be transferred to Ismaning. In the village the people had a gloomy foreboding, but only after the war did the affected families learn the truth.

This action had been stopped in 1941, mainly because of the protests of the church. This, as we know, excluded the Jews.

Chapter Thirty

The end of World War 2. Munich, a city of ruins.
The Allies advance to the German border.
Farmers help with any vehicle they have, to clear the rubble in Munich.
Dr. Josef Göbbels calls for total war.
Women, old men and boys are recruited. A last stand.
The Sippenhaft.
The more hopeless the fighting, the more fanatic the Nazis become.

By now it was a foregone conclusion that World War 2 was ending, but it was not an ending the Nazis would have wished for. Although the Allies had almost advanced to the German border, fighting still continued. And no news from Toni! The post offices were mainly run by old men, too old to be in the army, and women. Anni, who still lived with her two children in the upper rooms in our house, was one of the women who delivered the post. Every morning when she started work, the first thing she did was to go through the post looking whether she could find a letter from Toni. When she arrived home in the afternoon, mother was waiting, desperately hoping for positive news. Yet all the hope was in vain. Anni knew from her own experience how devastating the waiting could be. She mostly just shook her head.

The air-raids kept increasing with the advance of the Allies to the German border. One of their objectives was Munich, the city where National Socialism had started. Especially severe were the air-raids in the city in July 1944 and a few days before Christmas and then again in January 1945. Those air-raids reduced Munich to a city of ruins. In those nights it looked from Ismaning like the whole city was in flames. Ismaning was under enormous pressure. The fire brigade with its very young and very old members, all other men were in the war, had to be on continuous duty to try and stem this conflagration. In July 1944 an emergency service had been started in the village. All farmers who had some kind of vehicle with a trailer had to be available to save furniture and anything else that was still fit for use. They also had to free roads from rubble to make them usable. To add to all these difficult problems, to the hardship and worries, came the tyranny of Total War, which Josef Goebbels, Nazi propaganda minister, called for, after the fall of Stalingrad. He called for the inclusion of all German men from 16 to 60 years-of-age into the army.

Also any vehicle privately owned e.g. motorcycle or bicycle, had to be given up for the war effort. This included the N.S.U. Toni and his friend had bought before the war, when they were training. When my parents were notified by the police of the date when the N.S.U. was going to be picked up, Shorsh thought this was quite unfair and went to the police to object. But the inspector was sorry, but told him the matter was out of his hands and the following day the N.S.U. was picked up.

Also women were not exempt. On 19th September came the command that all the women from Ismaning born between 1920 and 1924 had to report to the Reichsarbeitsdienst (work duty for the Reich) within one week, unless they could prove that they were already working for the war effort.

Boys from the age of 15 years were recruited in a Wehrtüchtigungslager (military service camp). The young son of a farmer in Ismaning, not yet 16, was in February 1945, sent for this purpose to a camp in Holzkirchen, a village near Ismaning. There he was trained to use a rifle and above all the Bazooka. In March 1945 he was transferred to Haar, another village near Ismaning, for a medical examination to test his fitness for military service. As he truthfully stated that he was healthy, an officer from the recruiting board was standing by and interrupted him, shouting furiously that he knew the boy suffered from a severe stomach complaint and therefore would be unfit for active service. He made it sound as if that boy was so desperate to be a soldier that he was hiding his illness. The boy at once realised that this man was a philanthropist, who felt sorry for those boys, and tried whenever possible, to help those who were still practically children. Happy and relieved, that young farmer's son went back to Ismaning.

The Nazis wanted a replacement army. All men fit for service up to the age of 60 years had been drafted to the

Volkssturm (a German national militia), organised in the last months of WW2. They were reserve troops with military training. A last stand!

In spring of 1945, the Allies stood on German soil. Hitler's Empire, which should have reached from Nordkapp to Africa, from the Atlantic to the Volga, had collapsed!

German U-Boats and the German Luftwaffe could not stand up to the onslaught of the Allies. A great number of the towns were in ruins. In the last few weeks Dresden, a town already overcrowded with refugees from the East, and Würzburg known as the Lazaret Stadt (town of war hospitals), was almost completely destroyed. The war had once again taken on its infernal dimensions. The more hopeless the fighting was, the more fanatic the Nazis became. And still came the devastating news to families, that their father or son had been killed in action. It was the mayor's duty to deliver that letter. To some families he had to go twice. One farmer who was cutting wood on a circular saw when the mayor entered the yard for the second time, knew immediately the purpose of the mayor's visit, and in his utter devastation he went for the mayor, who very quickly took flight, with the farmer shouting after him that he was going to throw him into the circular saw, and a few other choice words, one of them 'Du Nazibandit' which I don't think needs translation. The farmer didn't care anymore. He was so devastated that he would have said exactly the same to the Gestapo. But no Gestapo came. So, obviously the mayor did not report him. I have never heard that the mayor ever reported anybody.

The fighting went on and the Nazis behaved more and more absurdly. Hitler's orders became evermore monstrous. From 5th February the Sippenhaft (liability of all the members of a family for the crimes of one member) was radically enforced. This meant that should anybody express an opinion not exactly to the agreement of the Nazis, and could not be seized, the family had to pay with all their possessions, freedom and very often with their lives.

On 15th February 1945 followed the introduction of the Drumhead court-martial. This was another escalation of the Nazi terror. It was a summary court for all criminal offences which could damage the German fighting strength. Up until now these offences had gone before a court martial. But now it was enough to express doubts on the final victory to be convicted. On 19th March, Hitler issued a decree that made his intentions quite clear: he wanted to deprive the Germans of every possibility of survival. All military transport and industrial infrastructure was to be destroyed. This did by no means mean that the fanaticism of the Nazis had come to an end. All men up to the age of 60 years of age had to join the Volkssturm (People's Defence) and were used as a kind of reserve for the last stand! The Nazis were still holding on to the hope and belief of a coming wonder weapon which would bring them the final victory.

Chapter Thirty One

The excitement of the last days of the war.
The onslaught of the Allies.
The village is in a great stir. People discuss the situation in the street. What will be the fate of the village?
The Volkssturm builds tank obstacles.
Will the village be defended as ordered by Hitler? Will the village become a combat zone?
The German pioneers destroy bridges.
Americans fire warning shots into the village.
SS men appear from the forest.

From 28th April, the excitement in the last days of the war increased. From 5 o'clock in the morning, on the news from all the Volksempfängern (radios) there were no longer any orders to hold out to the last soldier, no warnings of air-raids, and no Reichssender (Reich transmissions) from Munich, which had for 12 Years been used for Nazi propaganda. Instead came Freiheitsaktion von Bayern (Freedom Action of Bavaria) over the radio. For hours it pointed to the hopeless situation. The speaker started with: "Achtung! Achtung!" ("Attention! Attention!") "This is the Freedom Action of Bavaria. Workers protect your installations against sabotage by the Nazis. The Allies have entered Bavaria and are moving in the direction of Munich. Last night The Freiheitsaktion took over the Government, and the yoke of Nazi slavery has been thrown off." And the speaker asked the Wehrmacht (Army) to lay down their weapons. The resistance fighters under Captain Rupprecht Gerngross, previously the head of interpretation, stationed in Munich, were aware of Hitler's order that the bombed, starved, tired-of-war city should be defended to the last house. In charge of this plan stood Paul Giesler, the fanatical Gauleiter (the head of the Nazi administrative district) who had already arranged for 50 tons of explosives to be put on various bridges across the river Isar to hinder the advance of the American troops.

To save Munich, Captain Gerngross played a dangerous game. As quickly as possible he had to inform the advancing Americans of the existence of a resistance group, who was ready to hand the city over without a fight. They actually did manage to send the relevant message to the Allies, but now the Nazis managed to again take over the publishing house of the Völkischer Beobachter (the only national newspaper) and the Rathaus (Town Hall). In doing this the Nazis took some prisoners, yet Gerngross ordered his men not to use weapons. But without the Völkischer Beobachter, the Freiheits Aktion lost their power of speech. How could the Freiheits Action reach as many people as possible in Bavaria with their freedom message?

The solution was that the transmitter in Ismaning had to be captured. On the night of the 28th April, approximately 200 men of the freedom fighters marched from Freimann (a small town near Munich) in the direction of Ismaning. At 3 o'clock they arrived at the transmitter tower, overthrew the staff, and locked them up, and took over the radio station. From 5 o'clock until 11 o'clock a.m. the very surprised listeners heard the broadcast of the Freiheits Aktion Bayern, in German, French, English, and Russian. The appeal spoke of the hope that the German nation would once again become an equal member of civilised humanity. This message was not only heard in Munich, but in all Bavaria. At 11 o'clock, Captain Gerngross left the broadcasting station with his people to meet the Americans. Shortly afterwards, the SS marched into the station, however they were quickly relieved by members of the Volkssturm. The SS officers then disappeared quietly. On the morning of the 30th April once again appeared an SS Officer, whose orders were to destroy the whole broadcasting station. But he was tricked by the leading engineer, Herr Wolf. Already the noise of the oncoming tanks of the Americans could be heard. Herr Wolf gave the order to hoist the white flag, and the SS officer disappeared. At 4 o'clock in the afternoon the first American soldier entered the broadcasting station of American Military Radio Munich.

The inhabitants of Munich had a special interest when they heard on 28th April the appeal of the Freiheits Aktion Bayern. After all, the fate of their city was in the hands of a few. The people of Munich knew Hitler's orders: Munich had to be defended under all circumstances. This would have meant even more people dying. Six thousand had already lost their lives in air-raids. Two fifths of all buildings had been reduced to rubble. Therefore more and more of the inhabitants decided to wear white armbands and more and more white sheets appeared from the windows. Some very brave ones removed the explosive devises from the bridges. But for a last time Gauleiter Giesler wanted to show his power and contempt for mankind, when he ordered his troops to shoot anybody who was wearing a white armband. The order was not carried out. On 30th April the 7th US-Army entered Munich without a fight.

The city had been freed. The Freiheits Aktion Bayern had achieved their aim. The broadcasting station of Ismaning had played a far from insignificant role. Gauleiter Giesler fled to the so-called Alpen Festung (Fortress in the Alps) in Berchtesgaden, where he shot his wife and himself.

In 1947 a plaque was placed in the centre of Munich to remember the Freiheits Aktion Bayern, who saved Munich from the fate so many German towns and cities had to endure.

Then came 30th April 1945, the whole village was in a great stir. From the west and the north-west shooting from the advancing Americans could be heard, and to the south of Ismaning the Volkssturm was still building tank obstacles, which were quite ridiculous, the tanks would have just pushed them aside. Many people discussed the situation in the streets. Everybody wondered what the next hours would bring. Their main worry was the fate of the village. Was there a possibility that Ismaning would be handed over to the Americans without a fight, or would it be defended according to Hitler's orders, by the last troops of German soldiers. That would mean the village would be a combat zone.

Suddenly an explosion was heard. The German pioneers had destroyed a bridge at the east of the village and on the same day they destroyed several other bridges, thus totally isolating Ismaning. All the roads leaving Ismaning had been cut off. At the same time the Americans fired from the west into the village and hit the paper mill. Some veterans from WW1 said that they suspected this to be a warning shot, to give the village people the opportunity to hoist a white flag. The soldiers in the first World War had done this and had given the people 3 hours. From the forest appeared, from time to time, very young SS men arduously dragging with them their ammunition and weapons. Anton Seidl, the landlord of the restaurant The Mill, opposite the church, talked to them and persuaded them to throw their weapons into the village brook and leave the village to the west before the last bridge was destroyed. To his surprise they accepted his advise and left, as did some more troops that followed. They counted approximately fifty men. Then an SS officer accompanied by some soldiers came and asked the landlord to hide him and his soldiers in the cellar of the restaurant for a few days. The landlord pleaded with him and asked him to go, so that Ismaning didn't become one of those villages that didn't capitulate and was then destroyed. What that would have meant was unthinkable. The officer showed understanding and followed the previous SS men. As he was walking away he called back: "As far as we are concerned, the village can be handed over!"

The village priest, along with Anton Seidl and some local farmers felt that it was now necessary to come to a decision. Under no circumstances did they want any fighting at all in the village. They decided to hoist the white flag on the highest point of the village on the north side of the church tower, to make it visible to the approaching Americans. This dangerous task was carried out by Anton Seidl. But Ismaning was not yet saved. The word soon went around the village that the landlord of The Mill had hoisted the white flag. That quickly brought the leader of the Volkssturm on the scene, saying to the land lord:

"You have made great difficulties for me, for this treasonous act I would be within my rights to shoot you."

Soon more and more people joined and came to listen in, and in the ensuing tumult the landlord was able to disappear. He hid out on an isolated farm until the Americans entered the village. The white flag was exchanged for a flag with the Swastika; because rumours were still flying around that more SS men were hiding in the forest. Then promptly the Americans fired into the church tower and the water tower, which resulted in an enormous hole in both towers on the north side. Because the water tower was damaged we didn't have any water for three days. We had to fetch water in tin baths from wells in the forest.

Then another brave man again took the risk to hoist the white flag and this time it stayed until the Americans entered the village. By then any SS men and men from the Volkssturm had disappeared.

There was also another brave man, who must never be forgotten. Mr Hartl lived on Schlossfeld Strasse, in a small house with his wife and daughter. He mended radios, and he and his family led a very unassuming life. While the Americans were still stationed to the North of Ismaning, at Die Grüne Heide (The Green Heath, so called because it was heath land before it was inhabited) Mr. Hartl went around the village, on his bicycle, asking people not to shoot when the Americans entered. His intention was to ride on his bicycle to Die Grüne Heide to talk to the Americans to assure them that Ismaning would capitulate and not a shot would be fired. To the villagers he said:

"Please don't shoot at the Americans when they enter the village, if you do they will surly shoot me."

And so it was that the American troops rattled into Ismaning on 1st May 1945. Not a shot was fired, neither by the inhabitants nor by the Americans. Ismaning was surrendered, without incident, to the occupying Americans.

Partly apprehensive, partly relieved the inhabitants watched the exciting events through windows and from pavements. The war had ended in Ismaning after almost 6 years and so had the power of National Socialism.

Chapter Thirty Two

The Americans are billeted in the local school.
An American speaks German.

The American column entered Ismaning from the North and veered left by the Neuwirt (New Inn). Some people and children stood on the pavement watching the column slowly moving towards the schools where the Americans were billeted. I was one of those children. 10 years old, a small, thin girl wearing a flimsy dress and barefoot, long red hair, which I wore in plaits and my face full of freckles. In the summer most of us children went bare foot.

Suddenly the column stopped right in front of me, a young American soldier was sitting in the driver's seat of a jeep, with his elbow nonchalantly on the window looking at me. He had very dark eyes and I looked right into them. It can only have been a few seconds, but I became embarrassed, and out of embarrassment I said: "Sprechen Sie deutsch?" ("Do you speak German?")

To my utter amazement he answered: "Ja, ich spreche deutsch, ich spreche sehr gut deutsch, ich bin nicht weit von hier geboren." ("Yes I speak German, I speak German very well, I was born not far from here.")

I, still looking into his dark eyes exclaimed: "Sind sie wirklich?" ("Were you really?").

He smiled at me when he saw my astonishment and said: "Ja wirklich." ("Yes, really.").

This conversation can only have lasted a few seconds before the column moved on. I still wonder whether he remembered that thin little girl ever again.

With his left hand he gave me a slight wave, and I gave him a slight wave with my right hand. I didn't watch the whole column moving past, instead I walked home deep in thought. Normally I ran and hopped and skipped, as children do, but not this time. I kept wondering, why this young man was with the Americans if he was German. When I got home I told Shorsh about the incident, but he totally dismissed it, with the words: "Of course he was not German, he was having you on."

Now, I know that this was quite possible, but he might have fled Nazi Germany. I still wonder - why would he have lied to a little girl? What would have been the point?

Chapter Thirty Three

Ismaning and the concentration camps. The infamous death march.
Reports from some inhabitants of Ismaning.

Of course everybody knew of the existence of the concentration camp in Dachau, near Munich. Yet the threats of - Be quiet! Don't listen to a foreign radio station, don't speak to a foreign worker, otherwise you too will end up in Dachau! - were hanging over the population. Yet in the last days of the war, at the end of April 1945, many people in Ismaning saw for themselves the horrors of the concentration camps, mainly those people who lived on the road coming from Freising, a bishopric to the north of Ismaning; and those who lived on Aschheimer Strasse leading to the West, found themselves confronted with the horrors of the concentration camps.

As the German fronts collapsed towards the end of the war, the prisoners were transported to concentration camps away from the front, to the south. Especially shocking and distressing was the evacuation of 4,600 evacuees on 8th April 1945, when they were transported in a closed freight train from the notorious Buchenwald concentration camp. This train left Weimar and was aimlessly shunted around through Germany, and eventually arrived on 27th April in Dachau. Of the 4,600 prisoners 1,300 were still alive and dragged themselves with their last strength into the camp. Added to total malnutrition there was also typhoid. Two days later the Americans arrived and liberated them.

Infamous is also the death march from Dachau to the south, finally finishing in Toelz in the Alps. It cost many victims their lives. This road of suffering is now marked along the way by impressive memorials.

Just such horrific evacuation marches also touched Ismaning. Some of those groups of concentration camp prisoners came from KZ-Aussenstellen (smaller sub-branches of the main camps), dotted all over the district, which had been closed. Ismaning was already in a state of chaos through the destroyed bridges surrounding the village, now from the direction of Freising came columns of KZ prisoners who were aimlessly driven on by SS men.

A distant cousin, Leni Gutjahr, two years my senior, lived with her parents and siblings on Aschheimer Strasse. This was one of the streets where K.Z. prisoners were driven along. She still remembers those people in their distressing state.

A group of ragged, exhausted K.Z. prisoners, driven on by SS, passed their house, and what she saw made an indelible impression on her. Their naked feet were wrapped in newspaper and held together by bits of string. Her brother, Georg Prasch, witnessed another large evacuation march. Again a column moved from Freising Strasse in the direction of Aschheim. Why they tried to get to Aschheim I cannot say for certain. I can only assume that the SS guards had no knowledge of the destroyed bridges. Georg described that it was an endless column of hundreds of prisoners, who for hours, completely exhausted and bent over, dragged themselves past their house. His mother was very much moved to pity and put buckets of water with ladles on the side of the road, but one of the SS came to her and threatened to shoot her should those buckets not immediately disappear.

This description was confirmed in 1959, because of the inquiry of the French Grave Commission in Munich. The then Bürgermeister (mayor) Erich Zeitler, confirmed on 29th April 1952 that from the direction of Freising a column of concentration prisoners had appeared on foot. There were approximately 350 to 400 men, who were to rest in the gym hall, in the Hain (the village park) in the middle of Ismaning, and then move on to Ebersberg, a town north-west of Ismaning. But the group of SS men disbanded.

To the question whether on the march through Ismaning, prisoners had died or had been shot or even bludgeoned to death, the answer is, yes. Those who died were buried in the local cemetery.

Rosa Miller, who lived in Freising Strasse, had a somewhat longer contact with the prisoners. She experienced how the prisoners from Buchenwald arrived in Ismaning and stayed until the end of the war. In detail, she described how approximately 100 prisoners dragged themselves from

Freising to Ismaning and stayed the night on the football pitch. The following day they were moved on and finally stopped in the Hain. They were guarded by one SS officer. A day later, on the 1st May, the tanks of the Americans rolled towards Ismaning. This day brought freedom for the compulsory workers and K.Z. prisoners.

The French prisoners of war had left the Hain as quickly as possible, where they had spent the nights for the last 4 years under guard, during the day they had to work. Before that this proud gym hall was the meeting place of the Hitler's Youth.

For the time being the prisoners from Buchenwald found themselves confronted by a helpless situation, as their guard, the SS officer gave himself up to the Americans. But in a very short time a help action was formed. The organiser was the well known philanthropist and opponent of the National Socialism (NS) regime, Joseph Sixt. His wife, with a group of ladies, decided to help these people. These were ladies who refused to join any organisation that had anything to do with the Nazis, and thus they became very unpopular with the regime.

Their aim was to help those completely starved, dirty and frightened people, as best as possible. The gym hall in the Hain served as accommodation. The leading ladies of the former NS Frauenschaft (Nazi women's committee) had to do the cleaning. Joseph Sixt organised enough beds and the right nourishment. The owner of the Neuwirt undertook this task. The local dairy delivered milk and butter, and a local baker the necessary bread. A special relief for these poor people was the public bathhouse near the Hain. A special dispensation of coupons from the Bügermeister took care of some cooking utensils.

In those first days, Frau Miller had the opportunity to converse with the SS officer who had to guard the Buchenwalder (prisoners from Buchenwald) on their march. Once he had surrendered to the Americans, he had to report to them three times per week. She experienced a broken man, who could not cope any longer with the reality of the NS regime. The picture of the many dead people along the evacuation routes would not leave his mind. After he was finally imprisoned in Moosburg, a town to the north of Ismaning, he took his own life.

In spite of all the efforts of private and council help and care, the Buchenwalder suffered a terrible setback. Typhoid had broken out and not only did the KZ prisoners suffer from this terrible illness, but the helpers were also afflicted. Frau Sixt, who cared from the beginning for these people, died of this illness. Then American ambulances picked up the Buchenwalder and transported them to their hospitals. These pitiful people will always be remembered in Ismaning.

The former KZ prisoners who died in Ismaning were collectively buried in the local cemetery. A flat, rectangular, stone slab with commemorative writing marked the grave until 1958. It was then that the bodies were exhumed and transported to the KZ Ehrenfriedhof (KZ Cemetery of Honour), in Flossenbürg.

Chapter Thirty Four

Ismaning after the war. Americans appoint a Major and Deputy.
The village is plundered by its own people and freed foreign
prisoners.
People are killed for a bicycle.
An MP looks for a friend of my family.
House searches happen daily for the first week.
The German army blanket.
The man without a face.

In the first weeks in May 1945, utter chaos reigned in the
village. The Americans appointed two men from the village
as Mayor and Deputy Mayor, who tried without delay to
establish order in the village. The ex-Mayor, father's former
friend Koorby, was arrested as all other known Nazis.
Koorby's daughter came to see my father in a very worried
state, and told him that her father had been arrested and
thought that the Americans would hang him. Very
convincingly Father managed to allay her fears, by saying:

"Why should they hang him, he never reported
anybody, and I am quite sure that he could have done, all he
ever did was shout Heil Hitler, and that we all did, because
we all wanted to go on living. Don't worry, they will soon
check him out and then they'll let him go home."

Which they did, but not before they stuck him on a jeep
in front of the wind screen and paraded him around the
village, telling the inhabitants: "Whoever wants to spit at him
can do so."

I haven't heard of anybody that did. After three days he
was home again. And as before the war, he continued to
mend watches in his kitchen. There was one Nazi who did not
enrich himself. Many years after the war I once mentioned
that in a conversation with a local woman.   "Ah," she
said. "He did well out of the farmers."

To which I answered: "Didn't we all, what would we
have done without the farmers?"

As an old man, Koorby used to go for walks in the
Schloss Park, where I once met him and greeted him. He
looked up asking: "Do you know me?"

155

"Yes, I do." I answered. "I am the daughter of Huber Shorsh."

His face lit up as he said: "Ah, you must be the youngest one. What's your name?"

"I am Lisa." I enlightened him.

"Yes, I remember now!" He exclaimed, and we parted saying good-bye.

But that was a long time after the war, when it was a pleasure again to walk in the park.

But in May 1945 the two Bürgermeisters and the Americans tried their best to bring order into the chaos. On the trees and notice boards the Americans tried to make the public aware that the American Military Government would discipline anybody who transgressed. But in spite of all that, the village was heavily plundered. Many businesses from Munich had stored their wares in local storerooms, to save them from bombs. Yet people knew and raided those shops and looted. They found fabric, shoes, luxury foods, and much wine and schnapps. And a lot of the loot was wasted. It was anarchy. People grabbed anything, and came away with perhaps one shoe of one size and a second shoe of another size. One person would pull something out of the hands of another person. It was even worse when they discovered the stored wine and schnapps. Barrels had been broken open and the wine was flowing freely and people drinking and still drinking even in their drunken state, falling over and crawling around in the wine. How quickly that strict discipline of the Third Reich had evaporated. And yet in all that chaos could be found a group of people risking their health and even life to help those less fortunate than themselves.

The Bürgermeister sent a petition for help to the American Military Government informing them that Ismaning, 14 km from the centre of Munich, was being repeatedly plundered. Especially threatened was the part of the village in the direction of Garching, a town across the River Isar (the same Garching where my father had gone begging, when it was still a village). Help was urgently needed. To stop these riots some men from the village formed a militia who hurriedly had to meet at the schoolyard when the siren sounded.

There were still prisoners of war from Poland in the village. Transport was very slow and it took a considerable time before one could think of going anywhere by either train or car. Any person lucky enough to get transport found it on the back of a lorry. Bicycles were a pure luxury, whoever had a bicycle felt rich.

The ex-prisoners of war would stop anyone on a bicycle and take it, and it was very wise to hand it over, as it didn't take much to get killed, which happened to one very young man. After they had been treated so badly by some of the Germans, they thought nothing of killing a German. This young man, Martin Ostermeier, was coming from the direction of Munich-Freimann, on the west side of the river Isar, he got as far as the Moll Bridge to cross the river, and there he was killed. His bicycle was never seen again. After four days he was found floating in the river. To cross the Moll Bridge was the only way to get to Munich, as it was the only bridge that hadn't been blown up by the Volkssturm.

Hans Wild, a very good friend of my family, had an extremely lucky escape. He too was on his bicycle and coming from Munich-Freimann, he crossed the Moll Bridge where two men tried to stop him. He had a rusty old revolver in his trouser pocket. It didn't work, but it looked the part. He slowed down, pulled out his revolver, pointed it at them, and sped away. By the time those would-be robbers had recovered from their shock, Hans was well away.

A few days later he and his sister were coming from Munich, still taking the same road, as they had to. Hans instructed his sister that in case they were stopped, she should carry on very quickly, and he would take his revolver out and do the same as a few days before.

Sure enough two men tried to stop them. Betty, his sister, cycled as fast as she could and Hans took out his revolver, pointed it at them, but this time those two were prepared and fired two shots at him. Luckily their aim wasn't all that good, Hans got off his bicycle threw it on the ground and walked off, expecting to be shot in the back. But they let him live and he walked home. That evening Hans went to his local, The Post, and there those two men were sitting as bold as brass looking at him smiling. Hans lost his temper, again pulled his revolver out of his pocket pointing it at them. He knew he couldn't shoot them, but at least he thought he could frighten them. The next thing that happened, two MPs came through the door. Hans knew he was in for it, ran to the back, through the kitchen and out and away. For three days he had to hide as the MPs were looking for him. Those two men denied having stolen his bicycle. Hans's crime was that he was in possession of a weapon, because as soon as the Americans came to Ismaning a proclamation had been made that all weapons, as well as binoculars, cameras, and photos of soldiers or Hitler, anything to do with the Nazis, had to be delivered to the Council where they were destroyed.

Shorsh had a revolver, a 08 from his days in the army, he did not want the Americans to have, therefore he buried it in the garden. He also buried his and Toni's photos showing them in the German army uniform, which my parents had hanging up in the house.

About one week after entering the village, American soldiers came to make house searches, looking for weapons. It was quite obvious that it was their duty. They were such decent young men. They looked into a few drawers and then left again.

It was on one of those days when mother saw an American soldier walking along our road. She ran into the master bedroom, I ran after her. I could see she was frightened. She was tugging at the blanket on her bed, pulled it off and through it at me, telling me:

"Throw it out of the window. Quickly, throw it out of the window."

"Why?" I asked. "Why?"

In a complete panic she hissed at me: "Don't ask, do it."

While she was straightening the bed again, I took the blanket and threw it out of the window, on the west side of the house. I had no idea why I had to do this and hoped nobody would see me. I found the whole thing somewhat embarrassing. I didn't want anybody to ask me why I threw a blanket out of the window. Then as if nothing at all had happened she walked back into the kitchen and we didn't have to wait many minutes when a knock came at the door and a young American soldier entered. We knew at once he had to make a house search. It wasn't much of a search. He looked in a few drawers and left, he even said: "Thank you."

Mother did appreciate that and said: "He was a nice young man, wasn't he?"

But she didn't trust him, however nice he was. Watching as he went, she made quite sure he was really gone, before she told me to fetch the blanket back in. It was a German army blanket which Shorsh had brought home, she had suddenly remembered it and thought if that soldier went into the bedroom and saw it, she most certainly would be punished for not having given it up. Father and Shorsh couldn't stop laughing when I told them. That blanket was dyed maroon and became an overcoat for me.

A man without a face, this is a man I remember and I still pray for.

Plundering was still going on. On one of those days my mother was told by a friend or neighbour that we could get a jar of jam without a ration card. Of course it would not have been real jam, but some jellidified juice. But perhaps it would be sweet, that alone would have made it worth having. We could get it at a grocer's called Gröbmeier, so mother's friend said. The shop was about 10 minutes walk from where we lived. Mother thought perhaps it would make a welcome change for Emil and myself to have some jam instead of sugar beet syrup. At first I was happy to go, until I came to the main road. There I met Shorsh on father's old bicycle. He stopped and asked me where I was going and while I was telling him I had the most eerie feeling of foreboding. I looked beyond Shorsh and looked through a very faint mist. I asked Shorsh: "Did you see that mist?"

Shorsh laughed and said: "What are you talking about, there is no mist, the sun is shining."

"But there was." I insisted. "It was suddenly a little hazy."

"Alright, it was." He gave in.

Then suddenly everything was unusually bright and crystal clear. There was Shorsh on father's bicycle, wearing light brown sandals, and I was frightened and tried to persuade him to come with me, but he dismissed my fear and tried to convince me that there was absolutely nothing to be frightened of and tried to make light of it. He said:

"Go on and get your jam, then we can all have coffee and a piece of bread with jam on it."

That convinced me that everything would be all right.

When I got to the shop the lady who served told me that my mother was mistaken and that there was no jam for sale. While she was still talking we heard two shots. The assistant quickly closed the large green shutters and the door on the inside. I and the other customers who were in the shop at the time with me, waited a while. But apart from those two shots everything was quiet. Gingerly the assistant opened the door and as we still heard no sound, she also opened the shutters and we all started to make our way home. As I got as far as the Neuwirt at the corner, I saw a group of people standing around in a circle. I was curious what they might be looking at. Somehow they didn't even notice me. I squeezed through and stood in front of the figure of a man lying on the ground. For a moment I stopped breathing. Something took my breath away. It was the same feeling as when sometimes a strong gust of wind hits ones face and takes ones breath away. Then my chest started heaving and I started taking breaths one after the other. For what I saw was something so pitiful, so horrific, so unbelievably cruel, that even now it is hard to describe. The man's face was unrecognisable. It was like a balloon, red, black and blue. He was not dead; he somehow moved his right hand. And as I always was looking for my handkerchief I assumed he was looking for his. I didn't have mine with me, so I couldn't give it to him, which I wanted to do so dearly. I then left that circle backwards and still nobody seemed to notice me. I ran home, barefoot of course and out of breath, I arrived at home and cried so bitterly that I couldn't tell my mother about the man. My whole body was trembling. Then Shorsh came in and asked: "Why is she crying?"

Mother answered: "I don't know, she keeps saying: He wasn't dead."

"Oh, no!" He said. "She didn't see that man? Did she?"

Here mother became really frustrated and irritated.

"Not you, too? Now tell me what she saw!"

He told her about the man, that he was Polish and had been looting, and the people caught him and beat him to death, with sticks, fence posts and anything else they could use.

About one year later I heard Mr. Sixt telling Shorsh exactly what had happened. That man had been looting and he, Mr Sixt, realised that a crowd was gathering and decided to take the man into the police station, thinking he would be safe there. But the crowd became more and more threatening and the man was straining to get away and in the end he had to let him go, but the crowd caught up with him and behaved, I cannot describe how.

I shall never forget him and I shall never stop praying for him.

Who was it that said - Civilisation is only skin deep ? And indeed it is!

Chapter Thirty Five

The Masters of the village.
A friend with the patience of a saint.
The Americans and the local doctor.
American soldiers and children.
Women washed for American soldiers.
The tragic death of Heine, my cousin's Polish boyfriend.

From May until August 1945, the Americans had become the rulers of the village. They had been billeted in both the schools, the boys' and the girls' school, which meant that for months we children had no lessons.

On the instructions of the commanding US Captain, who felt it necessary, again and again, to order the council administration to order the public not to try and seek contact with the American soldiers. Yet the captain did not succeed in this. The American chocolate, and the until-then unknown chewing gum, as well as exotic fruits, proved too tempting. Also American soap was very welcome. The soldiers soon noticed that it was impossible for the public to buy soap. Soon a trade started to develop. The housewives noticed that the soldiers needed their laundry washed, and the soldiers realised they could pay with a bar of soap or two, and sometimes also with a bar of chocolate for the children. This seems very poor payment in deed, and I think it was. To wash and iron a bundle of laundry by hand (washing machines did not exist) for a bar of soap or two and perhaps a bar of chocolate, this sounds unbelievable in 2012. But if a bar of soap becomes a valuable commodity, which it did, then it was good payment.

One day it happened that I passed by the girls' school when a young soldier came out and pushed a bundle of laundry under my arm and indicated to go home and said: "To Mama."

He had no idea what a position he put me in. My mother did not wash for the Americans. I think for some reason she blamed the Americans that we still hadn't heard anything from Toni. I think she was looking for somebody to blame. She used to say:

"The Americans should wash their own dirty laundry; I don't need their soap I can make it myself."

And she did. From the local butcher she would receive very old stinking bones, which were unusable even for cooking soup. She used some kind of acid and water, I cannot remember if she used anything else, and boiled it on the kitchen stove. All I remember is that in spite of opening windows and doors, the smell in the house was unbearable and we preferred to stay outside. But the result was amazing. Once the mixture cooled down, mother skimmed off the foam and ladled the rest into tins where it became quite hard so that she could cut it into bars. It was good soap for those days, considering that we couldn't buy soap, even neighbours came begging for a bar of soap. She also made black shoe polish, with soot from the cooking range and turpentine, here too, I cannot remember what else she used. My mother became very resourceful. People generally did. We lived from one day to the next. Every day was a fight for existence.

As mother was so resourceful, she did not find it necessary to wash for the Americans. And there came I, trotting down the road with a bundle of dirty laundry under my arm, when Fanni, as she was called (Franziska Wäsler was her full name) saw me and said: "I didn't know that your mother washed for the Americans?"

"Oh, Fanni," I said full of misery. "She doesn't. She will be ever so cross. The soldier simply gave it to me and told me to go home."

Full of pity she said: "Oh, give it here, I'll wash it."

Then I was worried and said: "But you don't know the soldier who gave it to me."

But she wouldn't let a trifle like that worry her. "Don't worry, they'll sort it out themselves."

That lady was a real saint. Nothing was ever too much for her and nothing ever seemed to worry her. Except once, even she with all her calm nature happened to be out of her mind with worry. That was when some boys brought her youngest daughter, Irmgard, home with both her wrists broken as well as her left upper arm. Some of the older boys had fixed a rope a thick branch of a tree in the forest. It hung over a large hole in the ground. Children used the rope to swing over the hole, as a game. But the rope became twisted round the tree and was not long enough to reach the other side of the hole. One boy told Irmgard to stop swinging as the rope was too short and she wouldn't get to the other side. But little Irmgard was a stubborn little thing and determined to get her way, started swinging, but the rope was not long enough to reach. It slipped out of Irmgard's hands and she fell into the hole. The boys managed to haul her out and take her home, with both her wrists broken as well as her left upper arm. Fanni was beside herself with worry. Irmgard had to spend 6 weeks in hospital at a time when visiting was most difficult, and on top of all that, Fanni still had eight children at home to look after. This she managed with the patience of a saint. All her children grew up and became respected members of the community.

But for now we are still in the year 1945 and the military rule of the Americans was felt in many various ways. Nobody could leave the village without an official permit. To this physical restriction, martial law was introduced. At first from 7 o'clock p.m. and later on from 8 o'clock p.m. nobody was permitted to be on the road. Anybody in violation of this law would be dealt with using the utmost severity; that was the announcement on 20th June 1945. We never did find out what they would have done had anybody broken this law. But the intrepid Doctor Josef Schmitt, the village GP at that time, broke the martial law when he was called to an American officer who was in need of medical assistance. Dr. Schmitt bravely made it a condition:

"If I can leave my house now, after curfew, to treat an American Officer, then I will also leave it to treat my own patients in the village."

Subsequently he received permission to do so. It also helped that the American Officer recovered very quickly.

Gradually the relationship between the Americans and the inhabitants of the village became more relaxed. Very often American soldiers could be seen after 8 o'clock p.m. patrolling the village by jeep and were no longer feared by the inhabitants.

Children hung around the schools in the hope of receiving little titbits from the soldiers. Our favourite was the boys' school, because that's where the kitchen was housed. I say our, because I was one of those children. The cooks were mainly polish, ex-prisoners of war who as yet were unable to go home, transport was the main problem. One evening when I was hanging around the school, a young polish cook motioned me to go round to the back, which I did. The village brook ran past the back of the school, I stood on the bank about a minute wondering why he had wanted me to go there. I soon knew when he came out holding a tin, but he was on the opposite bank. Stretching his arms out he tried to pass it over to me. I too stretched my arms out and I managed to take it from him. It was very heavy; it must have contained at least two or three litres. It was warm, without a lid, and I saw about an inch of fat swimming on the top. Real fat! Something I wasn't used to seeing. Full of joy I went home and entered the kitchen. Mother asked full of curiosity: "What have you got here?"

I was glad to hand it over to her saying: "I don't know what it is, but it looks and smells very good!"

And it was. Mother stirred it and and it turned out to be a thick broth with potatoes and vegetables. That evening everybody in the house had a feast. We soon found out why that young polish cook was so kind to me. Heini, that was his name, was sweet on my beautiful cousin Loni. They had started going out together and Heini wanted to marry her, but first he wanted to go home. He promised faithfully that he would come back, but it was not as easy as either of them thought. Once back in Poland Heini was refused permission to go back to Bavaria. Yet he was determined to come back. He tried to flee and was shot at the border.

War never ends at any one day, but goes on and on.

Summer came and the former prisoners of war, the forced labourers, and freed prisoners gradually disappeared. At best they could go directly back to their country. Also the Americans left the village at the beginning of August 1945. Now the most important task was the restoration of the schools, as the occupying forces hadn't left the schools in pristine condition.

Chapter Thirty Six

The end of the war brings the nuns back.
3rd October 1945, school starts again.
Denazification of ex-party members.
Starvation reigns in all Germany.

The end of the war brought the Schulschwestern (School Sisters) back to the convent, which they had had to leave in 1939. This year, 1945, school started again in October, not in September as usual.

On 3rd October teachers and pupils collected very noisily outside the girls' school. Teachers were in very short supply due to Entnazifizierung (the denazification programme by the occupying forces), so the few available teachers had to teach in two or three shifts. Every German professional was a member of the N.S. Party. This by no means meant that every person with a profession was a convinced Nazi, but in the days of Nazi rule, as a professional person, you had to join the Party. The alternative would have been forced labour. Every day, as part of their Entnazifizierung, the 60 members of the Nationalist Party in our village had to cut wood, fill in trenches and craters, of which numerous existed in the fields at the perimeter of the village, to clear roads and work on road building. Here, too, they had no choice, and until 1946, every Saturday they had to line up for inspection. They had been obliged to join the National Party in order to be able to continue working in their profession and also to avoid a conviction and forced labour. But even now that the National Party no longer existed they ended doing forced labour anyway. At least they knew that there would be an end, and at least they could live in their own homes. This was the reason that it took years until school lessons ran smoothly again.

It proved to be a very labour intensive task for the Council to organise the repair of the war damage, especially the restoration of the destroyed bridges, without them Ismaning was to a large degree isolated. Most important was the restoration of the railway between Ismaning and Munich. This depended largely on the reconstruction of the bridge across the Isar canal, only then could the restoration of the railway begin; if the occupying authorities gave permission, work could be started in February 1946, and permission was granted.

The main post-war problem was the supply of food. Starvation reigned in all Germany. The lack of fertiliser, seeds, equipment and labourers made an adequate harvest impossible. Also the separation of the agrarian regions by the river Oder and Neisse in the east were immensely noticeable. The allocation on the ration cards was far below normal nutritional needs. A daily ration consisted of 700 calories as opposed to the normal 2,000 calories. The city dwellers searched through the forests around Munich to look for mushrooms, berries and from beechnuts managed to gain some oil. Bartering was blooming. Once the trains were in action again they transported people to the countryside in the hope of exchanging clothes, bed linen, toys and anything that might be desirable to the farmers, for butter, eggs, milk and anything else that was edible. But not always did they manage to take their treasures home. The controlling authorities proved to be without kindness or understanding. Those people who bartered successfully and received a sack or half a sack of cabbage, potatoes etc. had it taken away at the border of the village by the local police. I never did find out what happened to the produce that had been taken off those poor people. I think its anybody's guess. Then as people became wise to it, they would store their ware in the yard of some local inhabitants and collect it in small quantities. For example, people had permission to take one cabbage, a small amount of potatoes, two eggs, and for such small quantities they had to come either on their bicycle, if they had one, or by train, once the trains started running again. But if you are hungry then a trip of 15 km is something you gladly put up with. I so well remember the cabbage heaps behind the garden shed of our house. Another possibility to fight the hunger pangs was the black market. There was only one drawback, monetary value was extremely low, but if you had a great deal of it you could still buy something on the black market, on Möhl Strasse in Munich, for a pound of butter one had to pay well over 100 Reichsmark. Then an

English Pound Sterling was at least 20 Reichsmark, it could have been more.

The method of obtaining food became a battle. Ismaning was still, as always, the main producer of cabbage, yet the yield was only thirty percent of that of a normal year. Alas, through the irresponsible manners of the public, this pour yield diminished even further. The Cabbage Invasion as it was called by the local inhabitants of Ismaning. It was impossible for the farmers to keep watch over the whole expanse of the fields. They proved completely powerless against the nightly plundering. Threats to set farms alight and violence against farmers was an everyday occurrence.

The price offered for one cabbage was 5 Reichsmark. To stem this course of events and to save the harvest, the authorities felt compelled to ask the police to help with guarding the fields, so that the cabbages could be harvested without incident, and consumers could at least count on a ration of sauerkraut for the coming winter.

It was at this time that we children started going begging to the farmers, for bread in the morning and for milk in the evening. If nothing else, we did mostly receive a piece of bread, and always came home in the evening with some milk in our small pitchers. At 5 o'clock milking time, equipped with our pitchers, we invaded the local farmers. Yet sometimes not all of us managed to get some, we were just too many, and the farmers had to keep to a quota which they had to give up. There were two farmers I only visited when I could not get any milk and it was beginning to get late, those were the farmers mother strictly forbade me to go begging to. They were her friends, the Fisher Bauer and the Fruehauf Bauer. Mother used to say:

"They are very good to us. They always give us food when I help them out, we mustn't exploit their kindness."

But I did! At the end of an evening, when I still didn't have any milk, those were the farmers I knew would never send me away with my pitcher empty. I never told mother and they never told on me.

*Sister Maria Richlinda, who was our class 7
and 8 teacher*

Chapter Thirty Seven

And no news of Toni or cousin Sepp.
Sepp in a war hospital in Oslo, Toni in barracks near Trondheim.
Toni saved a train from disaster.
Toni became good friends with Karl and Walter.
Their nightly escapades.

And no news from Toni or our cousin Sepp. Sepp was still in a war hospital in Oslo, Toni still in barracks in Störn, a village near Trondheim. But now the Norwegians took over command. All German military personnel were interned. Yet, in the internment camp German officers still had command. As far as the soldiers were concerned, they didn't notice any change. Life just continued in its usual way. The officers saw to it that the discipline was not lacking. But of course there had to be somebody like Toni, although he was by no means the only one who did his best to beat the strict German discipline, after all the war was over and in no time they would be home. It was now June 1945 and the English had arrived, which made the soldiers think that it could only be a few weeks before everything was wound up and they could go home. So come evening, those young men, for strictly speaking they could no longer be called soldiers, tried their best to have as good a time as possible. One evening when Toni came back over the very bridge he should have been guarding some weeks before, he heard a peculiar noise. It was a rushing noise, there was a small river down there, but it was more than that. Toni knew that a train was due and went into the railway hut he had slept in before, took the lantern, lit it and went under the bridge to investigate. To his horror he saw that the embankment had given way and completely covered the tracks. Toni climbed over it and ran along the railway track swinging the lantern and the train managed to stop just before the mound of earth. The train driver jumped off the train and shook Toni's hand and accompanied it with a flood of words, which Toni didn't understand and just to be polite he said: "Ja, Ja, Ja." ("Yes, yes, yes.") And with his lantern went back to his barrack, but not before putting the lantern back into the railway hut. He didn't tell anybody, as he thought it would be wise to keep quiet. After all, he was not supposed to go out.

The next day all the soldiers had to fall in, with the German, English, and Norwegian officers present. Toni was called to come forward. Here we go again, he thought, that train driver must have given me away. To his complete surprise he received a bottle of wine, a packet of tobacco, two packets of cigarettes and two bars of chocolate, and all the officers saluted him. That was something Toni was not used to, he expected to be in trouble and that would have been normal for him, things were turning for the better he thought. But of course he had very little from his gifts, as it was natural for him to share them with his friends.

Eight days after this incident, the company had to fall in again, and this time it was not to receive a reward. Life had become easy and soldiers took advantage of the relaxed camp life. Especially the three friends, Toni, Karl and Walter. Anything one didn't think of, the other one most certainly did. They couldn't think of a reason why they shouldn't go out together. Together they had much more fun. But it did not take long for the officers in command to notice that those three friends usually couldn't be found in the evenings. All the soldiers went out sometimes, but not as frequently as the three friends. In the beginning they managed to be absent without being noticed, or so they thought. Then the whole company had to fall in again and the three friends found themselves confined to the camp because of misdemeanour. Toni was confined for 10 days, Karl and Walter for 21 days. Why Toni was only restricted for 10 days, he never knew. They couldn't go on their nightly escapades as they were closely observed, but that was the extent of their punishment, but they were separated. Toni was moved to another barrack.

Then a most peculiar thing happened when Walter went to the toilet one day and found two young officers working on the ceiling, but they quickly stopped when Walter entered. He wondered what they were doing and spied on them. He managed to observe them through a small crack in the door and saw that they unscrewed a small panel on the ceiling, but couldn't see anything else. When he told Karl, they went and did the same and found, in the gap between ceiling and roof, boxes of wine, Schnapps, and brandy. The next day Toni was looking for them and couldn't find them and asked the soldier who was on guard duty of their whereabouts, who then pointed to their bunk beds where they were lying blind drunk. When eventually they told Toni of their treasure trove, he lost no time in helping himself and carried 32 bottles in his rucksack, back to his barrack. Then Walter and Karl came up for discharge with the first group. There was great excitement and with all that alcohol they could have a wonderful farewell party. Especially now that discharge had started and they all thought: Next stop home!

Trainline in Störn where Toni averted a disaster

Chapter Thirty Eight

Toni's discharge. He thought: Next stop home!
The soldiers are tricked by the Allies.
Prisoner of war camp on the clay hill. The journey to Belford in
France. The march to the château.

On 14th July 1945 it was Toni's turn for his discharge, which
was administered by the English. He had nothing but
admiration for the English military. When he received his
discharge papers he could keep everything he possessed,
which wasn't excessive, apart from his uniform there was not
much he did possess. Some of the English soldiers asked
whether they could have certain things as keep sakes. One
soldier asked if he would give him his belt buckle, which had
the words engraved on it: Gott Mit Uns. (God with us). Toni
gladly handed it over, as he hated anything to do with the war
and the Nazis.

Soon Toni realised that whatever he had from the
German military, the English soldiers found desirable. Then
all the prisoners in his group gave whatever they had away to
the English soldiers and received corned beef, bread, razor
blades and chocolate. Toni could even give away his canteen
and cutlery and the medals he had with him. My parents had
some of his medals, those he had given away when he came
home. He wanted nothing to remember the German army by.
He felt cheated and disgusted. He had just finished his
training, had never worked in his profession, instead he was
forced to do something he hated, in countries he only knew
on maps and that not very well. As far as he was concerned,
the German army had cheated him out of years of his life.
Therefore it was no surprise that sometimes he was reckless,
lied and cheated the army whenever an opportunity presented
itself. He was very good looking and very charming and
knew how to use it. Here was a good Bavarian boy, had never
lied or cheated anyone and was taken by the German army
and tossed into a life of violence. And all he could think
about was to survive long enough to get home. This time had
now come, so he thought. He and a group of soldiers
embarked a ship for Halle an der Saale (Halle, on the river
Saale) in Germany. In Halle the Americans took over and

made the solemn promise that they would be transported by train to Baden Baden and there discharged, again. The German soldiers believed it! They saw no reason why they shouldn't believe it. After all, they had discharge papers in their pockets from the English military. But the next stop was not Baden Baden, but Kreuznach, on the French-German border. Here French military guards took over. That was when they realised that they had been tricked all along. This was how the Allies made sure that none of the German soldiers tried to escape and above all that they followed instructions. When the soldiers realised what was going on it was too late, far too late. If Toni had had any idea that they had all fallen for a trick, he would have been the one to try and escape, he would have taken any risk. Yet the outcome might have been by no means certain, he might have been caught and even shot on the run.

In Kreuznach, into every wagon, the French guard put a box of provisions, but no water. Every wagon was heavily guarded. When they asked what was going to happen to them, or where the next stop would be, the answer was to be quiet and was reinforced by having a gun pointed at them. Toni was inconsolable; he was convinced that somehow he could escape. But the soldiers in his company reasoned with him, hoping that in France it would not be too bad, and perhaps soon they could go home anyway; France was not too far away from Germany. Then the order was given to disembark and under close guard followed the march to a prisoner of war camp. To call it a camp would have been an embellishment. The march went up hill where they, for the first time, encountered barbed wire and the ground consisted of hard clay. That was all, no shelter just a large space encircled by barbed wire. The soldiers called this place Clay Hill. This hill became notorious. Many years afterwards I heard Toni and his friends, who he shared his imprisonment with, talk about this hellhole. Eight days, they spent on that clay hill, without food and very little water. One pipe provided some water intermittently, only when the guards felt it necessary to turn it on. Many soldiers died on that clay hill. The guard, mainly Alsatians and Moroccans, had fun shooting through the camp. The prisoners sitting on the ground found it reasonably safe, but the ones sitting on the latrines were not so lucky. The guards had fun taking pot shots at them. In general they enjoyed shooting through the camp. None of the surviving prisoners knew the names of the prisoners who died, as they only met at the start of the transport from Norway. The remaining prisoners never did find out whether the families of the soldiers that died had received notice of their tragic fate.

On Clay Hill Toni made two friends again and the three stayed friends all their lives. I have met both of them, Peter Fassnauer and Franz Leopold.

Then in the beginning of August 1945 came another journey by train and this time into France, to Belford. Very weakened they disembarked the train and to their astonishment they found a reception of civilians throwing rotten tomatoes and other rotten vegetables at them and this went on all the way to the château, which became their next prisoner of war camp. The civilians aired their anger the only way they could, and those prisoners were just there. They had never been to France, and they didn't want to be there now, the ones who were guilty were far away. But those prisoners happened to be German, and they were there. Nobody cared whether they had anything to do with the destruction of France, they were there and therefore they had to bear the wrath of the civilians.

Toni was assigned to work in the kitchen. Hurray! He thought. At last I can get some food. Not so! He had to peel potatoes under the eyes of a very conscientious guard with a ready hand to slap him in the face should he dare take a quick bite out of a potato. But one thing the prisoners appreciated was that they received water every lunchtime and evening. Sleeping accommodation consisted of a concrete floor in a garage.

Chapter Thirty Nine

A firm called Mischler making venetian blinds, asks for
German prisoners of war.
Little people with little power.
Mischler's architect picks them up every day.
Brutal guards become timid.
Mischler treats them with respect.
Toni cuts wood for Mischler.
Christmas 1945.

In September, Mischler, a large industrial firm that made
venetian blinds, requested workers from the château to help
in the factory, as at the end of the war the firm was inundated
with work. The administration of this firm knew that the
German prisoners had to help with building up France again
and were not to be starved to death. But as it always
transpires, little people with a little power can prove very
dangerous. And the guards on the clay hill and in the château
only confirmed this. Toni, Sepp Fassnauer and Franz Leopold
at once offered their services. They had no idea what the
work would entail, but anything to get out of this château was
good enough for them. First of all they had to have their hair
cut and after that they had to be deloused. The delousing Toni
was not too keen on. It was done in a water bunker. It was a
hole filled with icy cold water in which the prisoners were
immersed. Toni managed amongst the confusion of all the
prisoners mingling around to join the prisoners that had
already been deloused, as he knew that he didn't have any
lice. Now sleeping accommodation, although still in the
garage, advanced slightly. The garage was fitted with bunk
beds, straw and blankets. Yet it wasn't all plain sailing, yes,
they had advanced from the concrete floor to bunk beds, but
now they had flees, which proved a minor inconvenience and
could easily be dealt with. Besides Toni, Sepp, and Franz,
several other prisoners had at the same time been allocated to
cut trees for local farmers, which was their first job, still
under the responsibility of the firm Mischler. Food and water
was available all day, something the prisoners could hardly
remember.

Mischler's architect collected them in the morning and took them back in the evening, promising to pick them up again the next morning. But as they had been lied to so many times they found it difficult to believe. They thought: Well, we've had one wonderful day, with more food than we could eat and water to drink whenever we felt thirsty. Yet to their surprise, come morning, the architect was there again to collect them. He told the men that Mischler had problems with the authorities regarding the prisoners from the château. He seemed to be angry as he said:

"I will collect you every day. Mischler wants you out of that château, and if they think we cannot have you, they cannot have you either."

Who they were, the men never did find out, and did not really care as long as it meant they could be out of that château every day. From then on life became tolerable. Now they had a guard to take them to and fro.

At weekends, one of the prisoners could stay in the camp to keep it tidy. Now the guards had changed from being brutal to being amiable, but never did they earn the respect of the prisoners who tended to ignore them.

The firm Mischler now had a free hand concerning the prisoners and treated them with respect and courtesy. Granted, they still couldn't give the prisoners the permission to write home, this was something only the government could decide, and the government was slow to act. But Mischler managed to get them out of that château to a prison camp in Fretigney. It was approaching December 1945, a bitterly cold winter and another Christmas not too far away. Toni was now working alone for farmers, mainly cutting wood, cutting Christmas trees, and although he received excellent treatment, this job did not contribute to lift his spirit. Here was a Bavarian boy to whom Christmas meant so much and yet he knew nothing of his family and they knew nothing of him. This time he could not decorate a Christmas tree with the bootlaces from his ski boots, as he had several years before and he did not even attempt to sing a Christmas carol. But Christmas could not be stopped from coming. From the French government the prisoners received the present they so dearly wished for. It was a double card to write home on.

Two cards joined together, separable by a perforation. Both cards showed the address of the camp with only one line to write on. Toni wrote: I am well, working for Mischler, hope you are well.

My parents received this card on 31st December 1945. To say that they were over the moon is an understatement. Not only the family, but also the whole street celebrated. The postmen waved the card all the way down the street. What a wonderful start to the year 1946 this was. My parents separated their card and on the other card they wrote: We are well, waiting for you to come home. And sent it straight back. This was our real Christmas, albeit a little late for us and for Toni. After three months the prisoners had permission to write letters. With the material he had available, he started to make yard brushes in the camp, whenever he had some time, to earn a little money. The prisoners had permission to go out for a restricted time. Toni only knew one word in French - Madame. He used to go to houses and farms addressing the lady of the house and in his Bavarian dialect he would say: "Madame, brauchst an bäsn?" ("Lady, do you need a broom?") With these words he would hold the broom in front of him. He always sold them. He did not receive much money, but he was happy with however much or little he received. Only once he didn't think the payment he received was enough. He went to a house, into the kitchen offering the lady his broom and she very kindly asked him to enter. He was pleased to do so and leaned the broom against the wall, next to the door. The lady offered him a chair by the kitchen table and poured him a glass of wine. Gratefully Toni drank it, thanked the lady and on the way out he picked up the broom and left. He didn't think the payment was quite enough. The lady was so astonished she let him leave with the broom.

Toni in France

Toni on the right, POW in France

Chapter Forty

Cousin Sepp.

The two cousins who had gone through the entire war together had to be separated at the end of it, as the frostbite on Sepp's feet was too deep. He became a patient on the hospital ship the Monte Rosa, anchored off Norway. On 6th May 1945 he was released from the Monte Rosa and transferred to the Akershus Fortress, into the hands of the English military. Following the relative luxury of the Monte Rosa it proved to be somewhat of a shock when his camp for two weeks was an ammunition depot. After that, some of the wounded prisoners were transferred to Drammen, a camp with medical facilities. Sepp stayed there until 18th August 1945 and then all the German prisoners with him embarked a ship to Bremerhaven on the North Sea. Hurray! All prisoners again thought: Next stop home.

Sepp was desperately lonely without Toni, more so as he had no idea where Toni was. He wondered if Toni had survived the turmoil of the last days of the war. If he hadn't, what would he say to his aunt and uncle, Toni's parents, when he arrived home on his own? He, too, believed that soon he would be at home. In this frame of mind he was not interested in making friends, he wanted to escape from everything associated with war and all he could think about was going home, and like everybody else, he, too, thought that day was not very far off. In Bremerhaven, the prisoners embarked a train to Ruedersheim, on the Rhine, across to Bingen and on to Brezenheim, near the notorious prisoner of war camp Bad Kreuznach. Thus far, the prisoners still came under the jurisdiction of the Americans.

On 1st September 1945 the French army assumed responsibility for the German prisoners and everything they had was taken from them. Amongst others Sepp had his canteen taken off him and the fork that came with it was broken in half. Now he had nothing but the by now, shabby looking German army uniform he stood up in. To Sepp it was no great loss, as every train would take him nearer home, so he thought. The first time he became alarmed was when they disembarked in Rotweil, and all the soldiers were marched into a prison camp and remained there for four weeks. After those four weeks, followed another train journey and this time the transport advanced nearer to the French border, to Tuttlingen. Now Sepp knew for certain he was not going home, but into another prison camp. Tuttlingen was a collection point for German prisoners, and here they were divided into groups. The group Sepp was in continued to Schönberg, near Berlin, where he had to work on lorries to collect ammunition. From here he was able to write home and there his mother (my aunt) and his cousin (my sister) who never passed on a challenge, managed to visit him and bring him some money.

During Christmas 1945, again he had problems with his feet. Through the heavy work and the cold weather the skin on his feet broke open. He was transported further to the south to a prison hospital in Biberach, which was occupied by the French Military. At least he thought now he was actually in the south of Germany. As soon as he was able to leave the hospital he was allocated less heavy work. It was wood cutting for families of the French military and making sure the families had sufficient coal in that particularly harsh winter. From the families he received respect and kindness. But he was still a prisoner. Every evening at 6 o'clock, a lorry collected the prisoners working for the families, to take them back to the camp.

On 17th February 1946, he could not bear it any longer, to be so near home and still be a prisoner. He attempted a very daring act. At midday he hid in a small bunker in the gasworks until 6 o'clock in the evening, and then started walking in the direction of Ulm, which was under the occupation of the French and the Americans. He knew very well if caught, he would most certainly be shot. He walked along the railway tracks and came to a track inspector's house. He knocked, but his knock was not answered. He knew somebody was in there, he had heard voices, but now everything was quiet. He knocked again and again. He needed help. It was going to be a bitterly cold night. Eventually somebody gingerly opened the door. A mother was alone with her children, as her husband was at work in

Biberach. She was very much afraid, but once she realised that he was an escaped German prisoner she did everything she could to help him. She gave him something to eat and apologised that it was not much, but it was all she could spare. She also gave him a blue overall from her husband, which was another layer over his uniform, besides it made him less conspicuous. He left at 11 o'clock at night, and walking again along the railway tracks, he came across a barn with hey, where he spent the night. In Ulm he managed to catch a train to Munich and arrived there on the 20th February in the afternoon at 3 o'clock. Made the short walk to the Volksbad (public swimming bath) where he borrowed a bicycle from a friend and 30 minutes later, to the absolute delight of his parents and his sister, arrived home.

But not everybody was delighted to see him. When he went to the council to report back and to be allocated a ration card, the mayor in no uncertain terms told him:

"Go back where you came from, I am not going to prison because of you."

Sepp found this harsh in the extreme, but then realised that this wasn't surprising, considering the regime under which the people had had to try and survive for many years. One look in the wrong direction could have meant a trip to a concentration camp.

The mayor had to cope with all the tumult of the end of the war, and an escaped prisoner of war was something he could not deal with. He literally was at the end of his tether. It was not animosity on his part, he did not know what to do with an escaped prisoner, and he was afraid of the military police, as we all were. Previous experiences proved difficult to brush aside.

After the welcome Sepp had received from the mayor, he didn't have the courage to go to Munich to the authorities and ask for a ration card, he was afraid he might be sent back to France. But all those fears turned out to be groundless. The mayor soon had a change of heart and Sepp did receive his ration card.

For the first few days at home, and after the reception he received from the mayor, Sepp became somewhat concerned, thinking that perhaps the French authorities might call him back. Yet this concern turned out to be unnecessary. The French authorities had to deal with a great number of prisoners and in the aftermath of a world war could not possibly have looked for one German soldier who successfully escaped. But Sepp took some time to get used to his freedom. On one occasion a jeep stopped in the road in front of his parent's house, and when Sepp saw it he ran out the back of the house, across a wheat field and lay on the ground. He thought that the Americans had come to pick him up and send him back to France, but his fear was quite groundless. His mother went to look for him and told him that his sister's Polish boyfriend had happened to come and see her and was driving a jeep, as he worked for the Americans. Gradually Sepp became used to his freedom and didn't run any longer when he saw a jeep.

Chapter Forty One

Ismaning and Coal.
The Prisoners in France.

In 1945 the inhabitants in Ismaning counted 4400, and were predominantly an agricultural population. In times of peace, something almost forgotten, beer was a most important beverage in Bavaria. But in the chaos after the war, the Wirtschaft sold Dünn Bier (thin beer), some people called it Molke (whey). I remember this Molke, it tasted of rotten fruit. The smokers had a hard time too. Coupons for cigarettes were very often exchanged for food. Men took to collecting cigarette ends thrown away by American soldiers, and used the tobacco from those throwaways to roll cigarettes for themselves. But help soon arrived from a botanical novelty. The tobacco plant soon grew on a massive scale in the gardens of the village, after the cabbage plants had been transplanted to the fields. The care and processing of the tobacco plant soon became the most important conversation with men.

Also, a great problem proved to be the supply of fuel. On 20th June 1945 the council announced that for the time being there would be no assignment of coal. Therefore it would be of no use to apply to the council for this commodity. This was a major blow for the village, not only was coal used for heating, but for cooking as well. The peat of Ismaning as well as the dried stalks of cabbages became very popular, but the soot produced by those cabbage stalks was hated by every housewife. In 1946 the shortage of coal was still desperate. School children very often had extra holidays because of fuel shortage. Then the council realised something had to be done, and the decision was taken to clear some of the timber stock in the forest. The condition was that from every household one male would have to work in the forest for 36 hours per week and bring his own tools. Only then, the individual household would have the right to claim the appropriate amount of wood. Soon the heavy work became lighter, when the foresters with power tools were employed. Yet it was not a case of help yourself, coupons were still necessary to be allocated the wood needed. Not only fuel was rationed, but also food and clothes were in equally short supply. Needless to say the council was not exactly generous in handing out those coupons, as it was completely impossible to provide the whole population with all necessities. Ration cards were still prioritised. The farmers did what they could, but they could not perform miracles.

Eventually the Allies had to realise that it could become dangerous to expose the German people to starvation any longer. In 1947 food parcels arrived from the American Welfare Care-Organisation. Doctors went to schools to examine children. Most of us were undernourished, then every child received a daily Schulspeisung (School Meal). It is difficult to imagine now, how ravenously we fell on those broths and rice puddings. There was one bar which was my favourite, it was called Hohberger Schulfruehstueck (Hohberger school breakfast) Hohberg was the providing firm. I know nothing else about this firm, but never did I forget their breakfast. It was a bar of pressed oats with sugar and sultanas. It tasted heavenly! It was small wonder that it was our favourite. It was sweet, wasn't it? Something we had not tasted for a long time. The only sugar I ever tasted was on my birthday, when I always got a spoon of sugar in my coffee at breakfast.

Then also, in 1947 General George Marshall went to Germany and met Dr. Konrad Adenauer, who became the first German Chancellor after World War 2, and the famous Marshall Plan was implemented. The Allies, the victors, gave the defeated nation a hand-out. But of course mistakes do happen, especially when two people, despite the best will in the world, and from different sides, try to communicate and aren't quite familiar with each other's language.

That's how it came about that the German people had to eat themselves through a mountain of dried maize.

General Marshall asked Dr. Adenauer what it was that the German people needed first of all. Dr. Adenauer said: "We need Korn." Korn is the collective word, in German, for grain. Yes, Germany was in desperate need of grain to produce flour. General Marshall's answer went something like this: "Corn you need, you can have as much corn as you like."

We didn't receive as much as we liked, we received a whole lot more. Dried maize was totally unknown in Bavaria. But it was there, what to do with it, but eat it? It was ground to flour, made into semolina and rice. We had tons of the stuff, and we had to eat it. But as it was unknown, people didn't know how to cook it. My mother did her best by trying to make semolina soufflé, rice pudding. I don't think I am exaggerating when I say – it was truly awful! Everything was yellow. My mother baked bread and rolls. Everything was so dry we found it difficult to swallow. It took several weeks before we had eaten ourselves through a mountain of corn.

On Sunday 1st June 1948, the worthless Reichsmark was changed into the Deutsch Mark. Whatever money people still had was now worthless. Every person received 40 Deutsch Mark. This was enough to buy food for one week, and the money they earned in that week helped to continue to buy food and anything else that was needed. Germany could import again. Now the German people could start living again and rebuilding.

While all this was going on in Germany, Toni was still a prisoner of war in France. In August Toni and his friend Sepp Fassnauer still worked for Mischler. They had permission to work without a guard. Then Sepp was transferred to Noirdonne. As an electrician, he was needed there. Toni had a room above Mischler's canteen and shared it now with Walter, another friend. Most of the older prisoners had already been released. The treatment Toni and Walter received was excellent, and what was particularly welcome was that they received a small salary. At weekends their pay was the same as that of French workmen. The highlight of it was the promise that they too would be released in December. Then the firm Mischler received a letter from the French Government that the two prisoners Toni and Walter had to return to the prison camp in Belfort. Mischler's architect took them in his car and promised not to go back to Fretigney, Haute-Saône, without them. He didn't think there was anything to worry about, as they would be released in December anyhow. As they arrived at the camp they found that many of their friends had arrived before them, and were as puzzled as Toni and Walter. They were soon to find out. The French government had decided that they needed those young professionals at least one year longer. But they did give them a choice. If those German prisoners would sign a contract to work in their profession for one more year they would be treated like civilians and receive the same salary, and could go home on holiday for three weeks. Should they decide not to sign the contract they would all have to work in coal mines. That was the choice! None of them believed that they would actually be permitted to have a holiday at home. But they signed the contract to work in France for one more year, because the alternative did not sound too attractive to those young men.

Yet true to their word, the French Government sent passes to all the firms who employed German prisoners. In December Walter, being older then Toni, had been released. Toni was now on his own and still waiting for his pass and became somewhat worried. He was supposed to go home at the end of December for three weeks. After all he had signed the contract to come back to France for another year. He went to Mischler's architect enquiring about the hold up of his pass. The architect looked at him for a moment, then said: "Sorry Toni, you are not going home."

At first Toni thought the architect was joking, and didn't think it was funny. He answered: "You don't mean that. I have signed the contract."

"Yes, you did." Came the reluctant answer. "And you will go home after one year, but not now. If you go home now, I am convinced that you will never come back."

Toni promised that he would come back, he even pleaded, saying:

"I know my reputation isn't that good, but I am not in the habit of breaking promises. You can believe me when I say that I will come back."

But the architect would not relent. Instead he said:

"I know you want to go home, you've talked of nothing else, but we need your skill, we cannot afford to let you go home."

Here Toni became angry and he shouted at the architect: "Would it have been better if I had made a mess of my work?"

But here the architect smiled saying:

"You could never have done that, I have watched you working, the way you take pride in your work, that's why we cannot let you go, we desperately need your skill."

Toni was so angry and shouted back:

"Believe me, if I had known what you had in mind for me, you couldn't imagine the mess I would have made of every brick I have laid."

The architect didn't trust him enough to believe him that after a holiday of three weeks in Ismaning, he would come back to France for another year. Still angry Toni went to his room sat on his bed and cried bitterly. What's more he blamed himself. Going home and what he would do was his favourite conversation. He felt alone in the world and all he could do was sob his heart out. But that didn't last very long. Suddenly he realised that he had signed the contract, consequently he was no longer a prisoner but a civilian. The guards had all disappeared, he could have escaped, but what a homecoming that would have been! No that was not on the cards. He was a civilian and he would behave like a civilian. The next day he went to Vesoul, in the region of Franche-Comté, to the Prefecture responsible for German prisoners. He asked for the officer in charge and was received by a middle aged gentleman who offered him a seat and asked Toni for the reason of his visit. Now Toni had a very good reason to pour out his heart. Honestly, he told the officer about his reputation. He told him that he had lied and cheated in the German army, not because that was in his nature, simply because he hated the army, he hated the war, he had never wanted to go away from home in the first place. He never made a secret out of that.

"And now," he said, "I am the only one who is getting penalised."

The officer had a good answer for that.

"We need you to build up France again, after all you destroyed it."

Toni had an equally good answer when he said:

"I was not anywhere near France, I was up in the North of Finland having my feet frozen, the ones who destroyed your country are far away and left it to us to repair the damage."

The officer had to smile at Toni's quick answer, and he so well understood this young man. He told Toni that he himself had been a prisoner of war in Germany, and all he could think about was going home. Then he gave Toni the best Christmas present anyone could have given him. That officer gave him a pass to go home for three weeks after Christmas. Toni couldn't thank him enough and promised faithfully that he would come back and work one more year in France. To Toni's surprise the officer said:

"I know you will come back, and do you know why I am so sure?"

Toni just looked at him in surprise.

"I'll tell you." The officer continued. "You showed such determination and such desperation to get home, you will never jeopardise this."

When he arrived back in Fretigney and showed the pass to the architect, that gentleman could only laugh and he said:

"I knew you would do something like that, but I tell you one thing, if you don't come back I shall personally come and get you!"

Now it was Toni's turn to laugh, and all he said was: "Just you wait and see."

In January 1948 Toni was permitted to go home for three weeks. He came home to a hero's welcome. The whole road was lined with people to welcome him. My parents festooned the front door with a garland and a sign saying: Welcome home Toni. The three weeks went like three minutes. He had hardly arrived, then he had to leave again. Father said: "I thought he would come for three weeks, we have barely seen him."

That was true, as the invitations came thick and fast. He didn't have a whole day at home. It was not surprising as people wanted to entertain him, knowing that soon he would have to leave the village again. But Toni wouldn't have been Toni if he didn't try something. After his three weeks holiday he went to the French embassy in Munich and told the official there that he had to go back to France, showed him the contract saying:

"I have no money left to pay the train fare, but I have to go back, so please could you arrange for me to receive the train fare."

The official very politely, but quite emphatically told him there was no way the embassy could give him any money. Toni had no intention to give up that easily: "Well, I can't go back then." Thinking now the embassy would pay. But the official wasn't disturbed by that and only said in his broken Bavarian: "Ah, Kopf reiss nix ab." ("Ah, you won't lose your head over this.")

Sepp our cousin, who had escaped from the French in 1945 asked Toni: "What would happen if you didn't go back?"

Toni thought for a moment, but then remembered what the architect had said, and told Sepp that the architect promised to fetch him back.

"Would he really do that?" asked Sepp.

Toni wasn't sure, but he had to admit:

"He might just do that, as he was not very pleased that I received permission to go. Besides he was so sure that I wouldn't go back, therefore I think I'd better prove him wrong."

But he did stay four weeks instead of three and went back to Fretigney on 1st February 1948.

That year went faster for Toni then any of the previous years he spent in France. True to their word, the French government treated him like a civilian and he earned as well as any French man in his profession. The firm Mischler always did treat him with respect, already when he was a prisoner.

In March 1949 he came home and this time for good. Again he made everybody in the village look at him with astonishment. He didn't come home empty handed; he was actually pushing a yellow racing bicycle, which he had bought in France. He couldn't have attracted more attention if he had come home with a Porsche.

Young men and boys were standing around him admiring his racer as they called it. He was asked again and again: "Toni, can I have a go on it?"

They all did. In 1949 a bicycle was something quite special in Ismaning, and a racer was something not even seen before. This racer is still going strong. His son in law is now the proud owner of it.

Toni received a reference from the firm Mischler, to prove that he had worked in his profession, as after his training he had never worked in Bavaria.

From May 1945, the surviving soldiers slowly came back. Very often after an immense walk, as all the transport had completely collapsed. Over 300 of the home-comers had health problems. Added to the physical pain was the psychological pain. They had been robbed of their youth.

The last young man to come home was Franz Hungerhuber. In 1940 he was conscripted into the German army, not to come home until 1955. The last 11 years he had to work in a mine in Siberia, near Karagonda, until the meeting with Dr. Adenauer, German Chancellor, and Nikita Chruschtschow, made it possible for him and other German prisoners to be released.

Ludwig Zott, the young man who used to live with his wife in my parent's house upstairs, was another prisoner who came back from Siberia and found it difficult to get used to his freedom. His wife used to find pieces of bread and sugar cubes inside his shoes and socks.

On 18th October 1955 the village gave Franz Hungerhuber a hero's welcome.

189 soldiers from Ismaning died in the war, and from the 81 young men missing in action nothing was heard of again.

Chapter Forty Two

Ismaning and the deportees from the Sudetenland.
Whoever said WW2 ended in May 1945? Not for the Germans
and not for the refugees from Czechoslovakia: the Forgotten
People.

The fighting might have stopped, but war is a monster that
doesn't give up its grip easily. To all the turmoil of post war,
with hunger and lack of material goods and psychological
problems came a new next-to-unsolvable problem. More than
1000 displaced people, predominantly from the Sudetenland,
who had to endure the hardship of being forced from their
home and country, and after a cruel journey, were forced to
live in a village they had never even heard of.

In the 12th and 13th century the King of Böhmen und
Mähren (Bohemia and Moravia) called on farmers, craftsmen
and traders from Germany to inhabit and develop border
territories. For centuries they had lived with the
Czechoslovakians, intermarried, and spoke each other's
language.

Shortly before the end of the war, the American army
marched into Czechoslovakia. Some weeks afterwards the
Americans cleared the region, in accordance with an
agreement, to leave the country to the Russians. Women and
girls had for some time to live in hiding, as rape and murder
were widespread in the Russian army. Now only Czechs
could work in public relations, and the acts of horror started.
The Germans found themselves without rights. Public
transport was out of bounds for them, medical treatment was
no longer guaranteed and the allocation of food was restricted
to a minimum. All objects of value had to be handed over,
even radios and all technical equipment of any kind and
bicycles. The growing fear of reprisals, imprisonment and
deportation were ever present. In the New Year 1945/46 it
gradually leaked out that all Germans, in accordance with the
Potsdam Agreement, would be deported. On 10th July 1946
five families from Neukaunitz, altogether 23 persons, were
deported. Only two hours before the deportation the order
came to appear at a collection point with luggage of 50 kilos
per person. But very often 50 kilos was all a family could

take, as children couldn't carry 50 kilos. Walter, a school friend and one of those deportees, when talking about those horrific times, said to me: "What child could carry 50 kg?"

At the collection point their luggage had been repeatedly searched and anything useful, including toys, had been confiscated. Only a few Germans with professional expertise had permission to stay. The train with of the rest of the people went to the evacuation camp in Tepl, a former concentration camp, and had to stay there for four weeks. Half of this camp was divided by barbed wire, and still had the watchtowers as used by the Nazis to watch over the previous occupants. The Germans were transported from all regions of Tepl to this camp. From here followed the arranging of the transport to various destinations. One was the Russian zone (later called DDR, Deutsche Demokratische Republik) and the other the Western zone. The food rations consisted of black coffee, mornings and evenings and a piece of bread, lunch was a kind of flour pudding. On 5th August 1946 transport No.11 went on its way, it consisted of sixty freight wagons, with 1211 persons. Late that evening this transport left Tepl in the direction of the Wiesau frontier in the American zone, in Bavaria. In the camp of Wiesau ensued the registering, examination and delousing and at last a meal. In the evening that day the journey continued over the bombed town of Regensburg, where at the train station every person received one litre of water. From there the train went into the transit camp, the notorious Dachau. The first thirty wagons went to Munich Ostbahnhof (East Train Station) and on to Perlach and stayed the night. In the morning the train went back to Munich Ostbahnhof and the occupants of the thirty wagons boarded buses that stood in readiness outside the train station to receive all the people, to take them on 8th August 1946 to Ismaning. Here they had to try and make a start with nothing.

Emmy Kaplan - An amazing lady

"When in May 1945 the war was over in Lichwe, Czechoslovakia, none of us knew what was going to happen to us. As soon as the Russians came, Martial law was declared and the Germans became fair game. The Russians entered the houses, mainly in the evenings, and drank their Vodka. Once my father had to slaughter a pig for them. While all this was happening, we three girls hid ourselves in the hay loft, where we spent many nights. The Russians stole bicycles, watches, and anything else they wanted. It was inevitable that in Lichwe casualties occurred. Often those girls and women who could not bear any longer a life of continuous rape preferred suicide; but even murder was nothing to attract the attention of the authorities. After my father refused to disclose the hiding place of his daughters, one drunken Russian shot him as well as the farm hand. On 10th May 1945, all men from Lichwe were arrested and transported to Auschwitz, but were released after four months. In July 1945, all owners of farms and houses were expelled. Within ten minutes everyone had to stand in the street and then assemble in a meadow, and from there we were marched into an empty factory. Every day Czech farmers chose useful Germans to help with the work on the farms. It was a real slave market. Into the farms had moved administrators, but only a few of them had any idea about farming and were glad when my mother helped with advice and work. The harassment kept increasing; now we had to wear yellow armbands to label us Germans. Thus they could identify us, as we were prohibited use of public transport. Should the need arise to use public transport, we had to be accompanied by a Czech. When I went to see my dead father, in the mortuary at the hospital, a former maid kindly accompanied me. It was also our duty to greet the Czech soldiers very politely. Only once I didn't do this, and in a rage the soldier went towards my mother shouting at her:

"If you want your daughter to keep her black hair, make sure that she greets us with respect!"

Because it was possible that otherwise my hair would be cut off, or even shaved off. With the Potsdam Conference (from17th until 2nd August 1945) came the expulsion. The manner of the expulsion was always the same: first the notification, then the instruction - how much luggage any one person was permitted to take. This depended entirely on the officer on duty, whether permission was given to take twenty, thirty or fifty kilos. The greatest harassment proved to be the physical inspection, when the women had to completely undress. It was also a great distress for the deportees when at this late stage Czechs went through their few belongings and took whatever they wanted. Then we were interned in a camp near Wildenschwert, near Nieder Lichwe. Meals consisted of meagre rations, and we had to sing Volks (folk) songs for the officer on duty. After three weeks in this camp we were loaded onto freight trains. Thirty persons with their luggage had to enter one wagon. The floor was covered with straw. Four days we lived in those wagons, with very little food, consisting of beet soup. On the few occasions when the wagons stopped and were opened, Czech soldiers with machine guns stood outside guarding the train.

The deportation as discussed in Potsdam became nothing but an illusion, or shall I say it became a lie.

The first train went on 16th February 1946 to Hessen. The second train, that was us, went at the beginning of April 1946 to Bavaria, where after days we arrived in Dachau. The 120 people from Lichwe arrived in April 1946 in Ismaning and were housed in the various guesthouses in Ismaning."

Edith Tomaschko

Here is another story told by Edith Tomaschko (Edith Zellner after marriage). Edith Tomaschko became my teacher for one year. She knew how much I admired her. Naturally the nuns attracted my first admiration. But Edith Tomaschko was the only secular teacher I ever admired enough to become my role model. She had everything a teacher could have in my eyes. She was very pretty and above all very clever. This young lady was very dedicated and tried to teach us everything she knew. She even taught us physics, but I didn't understand much of it. However some things I did understand and those things that I did understand I have never forgotten, and it started my interest in physics and I am still fascinated by it today.

But back to June 1946. A mother came with her 4 daughters to Ismaning from Budweis via Pilsen and Furth im Wald.

"For days we were, as all other deportees, shunted about in freight wagons and eventually arrived in Dachau. Journeys that should have taken hours took days. In Dachau we received a meal and as always followed the usual medical examinations with delousing."

Then back into the wagons and on towards Perlach near Munich, where Herr Deinwallner, a haulage contractor from Ismaning, waited with lorries to transport them to Ismaning.

"By now we all were so exhausted and with our senses numbed we climbed on to the lorries, not asking where our destination would be, or even where the next stop would be. Even if we had wanted to enquire it would have been no help to us, as we had no idea where we were, or for that matter where Ismaning was."

All together they counted fifty people from Budweis. It was a day teeming with rain when they arrived at the council premises in Ismaning. A window on the first floor opened and the deputy mayor called out:
"Why do you bring me so many people when we have so many already?"
The people, who through no fault of their own, had been thrown out of their homes and their country, had lost everything, had to hear this. But as once before when my cousin Sepp came home as an escaped prisoner of war, the mayor didn't know where to turn to. All those deportees had been forced into a devastated country, lacking food and accommodation. A number of evacuees from Munich, who lost their homes through bombs during the war, still lived in Ismaning.
But the deportees from the Sudetenland could not change the situation either. The deputy mayor expressed his frustration only because he was unable to fulfil his obligation towards the deportees.

Some of the locals too, let it be known that they disapproved of accommodating the deportees.

Here again it was a case of: they were just there. The people responsible were far away. From some of the inhabitants they had to tolerate being called Rucksack Germans or Gipsies, and more.

Yet I found it quite astonishing that every deportee was eager to talk to me and not one person bore any grudges towards the people of Ismaning despite their difficult beginning. Whenever I touched on those incidents they would say: "Oh, that was a long time ago."

And indeed it was. Now I think it is a good idea I let Edith Tomaschko tell her story.

"Eventually we received accommodation in the Gasthof zur Post (Guesthouse of the Post). There we found camp beds left behind by the Americans. Everyone was permitted to take a camp bed and in the big hall find some corner to sleep. Washing facilities were unavailable; instead the little brook running past the guesthouse had to serve for our morning wash. But the landlady had some understanding and then gave us the use of her laundry room.

One day we discovered the river Isar. It was a walk of 15 minutes through the forest. How happy we were to find this beautiful river with its clear water. From then on we washed ourselves in the Isar. The locals watched us with astonishment when we even washed our hair in the Isar. After four weeks the council decided that we should have a flat, but as our family comprised of five persons this proved to be somewhat of a problem. But we were allocated a flat in the Torfbahn (Peat Station). From here workmen used to go to the moors to cut peat for fuel. This was discontinued before WW2.

We could move into two rooms, not in the main building though, in the annex. The flat was situated on the ground floor and had a small porch. The whole flat was filled with unusable rubbish. My mother was heart-broken. The official responsible for our move into this flat saw how disconsolate my mother was and felt sorry for us, but he could do nothing to improve the situation. To give us some encouragement he said:

"You'll soon have it cleared up, and look you even have a cooker, you can cook and heat the rooms and you don't need to bother anybody."

With a faint smile he left. We looked around, looked at the cooker and had to realise, yes, we had a cooker - that was wonderful. To cook and heat the rooms he said. But what with? There was a lot of rubbish, but the flat was completely devoid of fuel, or any cooking utensils. All we had were bunk beds. In the main building lived a family who became not only our friends, but also our rescuers. Soon we were the proud owners of a table and chairs and two cooking pots, one for potatoes and one for cabbage. As time went on kind neighbours gave us two forks and two spoons. Now we could eat, not together, but two of us at a time, and gradually the situation improved.

But another big problem was looming ahead. We had neither wood nor coal, and winter was only a few months ahead. All we could do was collect wood in the forest and the local park. Once we found a fallen tree in the forest. It was not too heavy, but it still needed the three older girls of us to carry it. We managed to shoulder it and carry it home through the village. It was quite a show for the locals. Our good neighbours helped us again and lent us a saw, a cleaver and a wooden cart, which we used to pull our precious wood home in the future. Our time was mainly spent collecting wood in the forest. Mother used to stack it in the porch. Then it happened one day that we met the forester and in surprise he asked:

"And what do you think you are doing with that saw in the forest?"

We told him that we had to get wood from the forest just now before the winter, as we had a cooker for cooking and heating from the council, but no fuel whatsoever. What could we possibly do? At first he told us quite sternly: "I can't allow that!"

This brought us close to tears, as there was no other way we could have warmth at all in our flat with the winter so near. When we told him that, we could see a more tender expression spreading over his face, and with a kind and warm voice he arranged a day with us to go into the forest to cut two trees he would chose for us. He realised we were no thieves, only desperate. Our friendly neighbours helped us again and helped us to saw and split them. This way the wood was easy to transport. It took several journeys, which we gladly undertook. By now the porch had become somewhat crowded, as it was also the place where we stored potatoes and cabbages, the result of begging or sometimes procuring by other means.

Despite the wood we had, we still felt the bitter cold terribly in the winter of 1946/47. Ice crystals formed on the walls of our bedroom. In the following spring they fell on our beds. My aim and that of my sisters was to go back to the profession we had been trained for. I was a teacher. But I don't want to forget to mention the schoolmaster and rector, Herr Franz Richter, of the school in Ismaning from 1931 – 1945. He showed us young deported teachers a way to achieve our aim."

Class 6, immediately after the war.
Our class teacher, Edith Tomaschko, on the far left,
I am on the second row up, third from the right

When in September 1946 the new school year started, there arrived among the crowd in the school yard three new, very young and pretty teachers. One was Miss Edith Tomaschko from Budweis, the other two were Miss Emmy

Kaplan and Miss Elfriede Vinzens, from Lichwe. That gave the inhabitants of the village something to talk about.

The Family Wittmann
- Another arduous beginning in Ismaning

In 1946, families, again deportees form Neukaunitz, in the Egerland, in Czechoslovakia, arrived in Ismaning. They too had some stories to tell. This time somewhat different, but no less heartbreaking. The families Wittman, Hagn, Beck and Koehler and others from Reichenberg, counted thirty persons.

A personal report from the family Wittmann:

"After our arrival in Ismaning, with our few belongings, the council moved us into emergency accommodation, in the hall of the guesthouse Zur Mühle. Thirty people in one hall, albeit a large one, was difficult to say the least. To begin with we had the wooden floor and some benches to sleep on. Some days later the council provided us with some sacks, but we had to get our own straw. This meant going to farmers and begging for it. This beginning was the first contact we had with the local inhabitants. A few compassionate farmers gave us some straw to fill our sacks with, to make more comfortable sleeping arrangements. It was for us new comers and for the local inhabitants difficult to cope with the aftermath of the war. From the council we received ration cards, which were not nearly enough, especially for eating permanently in a guesthouse, as we did not have a cooker. We realised that we had to think of something, and poverty teaches one to be inventive. In the forest near the Isar, we found a large piece of tin. It had once served as a sign for a Munich brewery, and with this piece of tin we built a cooker, albeit a very primitive one, but at least we could cook something. In the Hain, the park with its gym hall, that once was the home for French prisoners of war, we dug a shallow hole and put the piece of tin on some bricks over it, there were plenty of bricks lying about, and we had a cooker. For the following weeks this proved to be a very precious object. The only difficulty was when we had a foggy day. The fire wouldn't burn very well, and it was difficult to see whether the water was boiling or not.

We had not much to cook and were deliriously happy when we could help the farmers with the harvest. For our work we received potatoes, cabbages and milk. Also by bartering with the few things we had left, we managed to get some food to satisfy our hunger. Begging was extremely difficult as it was not only us who knocked on the doors of farmhouses, but also the evacuees from the towns who had lost everything through the bombings, they too were hungry. Then the council requisitioned spare rooms from any family who owned a house, and had one. This came just in the nick of time: when the last deportees left the guesthouse it was already bitterly cold. Winter 1946/47 was approaching fast. One room had to be enough for one family. Cooking had to be done together with the owners of the house. At last, in August 1947, we received a coupon from the council for a cooker. We needed coupons for everything which could not be readily obtained. Now we could cook in our room. For bartering on the black market, which was by this time booming, we had nothing to offer.

Besides the fight for our daily bread, we tried desperately to find our relations and friends. To begin with nobody knew anything of their whereabouts. Then the German Red Cross stepped in, and with a list of missing family members and friends we could be united again."

Therese Hanke

A petite, 18 year-old deportee from Brünn, the capital of Böhmen und Mähren (Bohemia and Moravia), married, on 18th October 1952, our cousin Sepp, in Ismaning. The Catholic Priest, Franz Osner, who was with Toni and Sepp in Finland, performed the marriage ceremony. By now Therese was called Resl, after the Bavarian pronunciation.

All the deportees had different stories to tell, of which there are only a few here. Resl told me her story many years ago, also different, but no less harrowing. This is her story:

"In April 1945 the Russians marched into Brünn. As soon as they arrived, the German population was marched into an internment camp in Olmütz. The houses owned by Germans were immediately requisitioned. For six weeks the Czechoslovakians were permitted to do whatever they wanted with the Germans, and what they wanted were slaves.

Every morning they came to choose however many they wanted for work, regardless of age. Sometimes a son or husband who had come back from the war, having been released from captivity, was hung without trial in the camp. We all had to shout 'Heil Hitler! Du Sau!' (Heil Hitler! You pig!) while this was taking place.

I was chosen for work by a farmer and his wife from Teinitz, a village 12 km from Olmütz. I was extremely fortunate that the farmer and his wife were the kindest couple I could have hoped for. I could eat as much as I wanted.

Sometimes when I was permitted to see my mother and my three year old nephew Dieter, I could even smuggle some food into the camp for them. My mother had to look after Dieter as his mother Trudi, my sister, had been incarcerated, because she had been married to a German soldier, who had died in the war. After three months she was released and was permitted to follow her mother and her son into the camp in Olmütz, where she too had to work for local farmers. Then in March 1946, one evening at 5 o'clock, the camp occupants heard from the officer in charge that they had to get ready for deportation with their luggage of 50 kilos per family and report at the assembly point just outside the camp. As I was not an occupant of the camp in Olmütz, but worked for a farmer in Teinitz, I was told that I had to stay with the farmer I worked for. I was frantic and so were my mother and sister. They refused to go and said: "If Resl is not coming with us we'll hang ourselves!"

As their determination was so real the commandant of the camp gave permission for me to join them and little Dieter. Now we could stay together, which was very fortunate for us. Should I have had to stay behind my life would certainly have changed, but not for the better. The farmer and his wife I worked for took me by horse and cart to the camp in Olmütz and even gave me some food to take on the journey. They were both genuinely sad that I had to leave.

On the following day, at 6 o'clock in the morning, a lorry took us to the assembly point near Olmütz train station and it was there that we received half a sack of sugar and nothing else. After we questioned the commandant why we didn't receive anything else, his short answer was:

"You have no ration cards; consequently you don't receive anything else. Be glad that I gave you the sugar. You can eat again when you arrive, wherever that is."

And immediately pointed to his gun. That kept us all quiet, even the courageous ones became timid. After three days, all of us internees were loaded onto goods trains. All the people of the camp occupied forty wagons, one wagon housed twenty persons with luggage. Some of the women had babies and small children. Which direction the goods trains were taking was completely unknown to us. When the wagons clicked shut we asked each other: "Will it go to Siberia?"

We tried to look through small gaps of the wagons, but were none the wiser. Each wagon had buckets we could use for toilets. Czech soldiers accompanied the wagons. The journey took three weeks to Furth im Wald, in Germany, after our goods train had been numerous times shunted onto empty tracks to give priority to passenger trains. Shortly before the wagons entered Furth im Wald, the Czech soldiers opened the wagons to take the small children and babies who had died on this horrendous journey, from their mothers.

Only now we received some bread and soup. Weak and tired, we didn't even ask where we were heading, thinking the Czech soldiers would only show us their guns again. Then a short journey followed to the local train station and the American military took over. The first question:

"Did you receive any food?"

"Yes," we answered "some bread and soup, after three weeks!"

Now for the first time we could ask: "Where are we going?"

This time we did receive an answer. "To Bavaria, direction Munich-Allach." (A north-western borough of Munich).

"Where is that?" We asked each other.

Somebody said: "I think that is quite a big place, we should be all right there."

And again it was back into the wagons and all forty of them took us to the distribution centre, Munich-Allach. We stayed there one cold night, too tired to look at the surroundings, and not understanding where our destination would be. We huddled together, too tired to cry or to talk. The following morning lorries arrived to take the occupants of twenty wagons to Rosenheim, a town to the south of Munich, the rest of us in the other twenty wagons were destined for Ismaning.

Herr Deinwallner was the first of the haulage contractors to arrive and started to take as many of us deportees as he could onto his lorry. Again all we wanted to know was: Where are we going? And, how far is that?

The kind man tried to give us courage, telling us that it would barely take an hour's journey to Ismaning. The way he looked at us showed us how sorry he was to see us looking like vagabonds, only vagabonds wouldn't have been so totally devastated. We saw that he found it difficult to talk, and for a moment he didn't say anything. When eventually he started talking again he tried hard to sound confident.

"You are going to Ismaning, a village where you are going to live from now on. At least you can live in peace there, and life will be better then living with the Czechs and the Russians." We picked up our little bundles, climbed onto the lorry, and all the lorries with the people from twenty cattle wagons rattled through Munich, and rattle it was, as Munich was still a city in ruins. That's when we realised that the people here too had been suffering terribly.

As we arrived at the council premises, the Mayor saw us and tried to talk to us, but found it difficult to understand us. After the hardships we had been through we appeared a little tongue-tied. He also felt harassed as yet another lot of us arrived, and as he couldn't immediately understand us he came to the conclusion that we must be Czechs. Therefore he became angry and said to the drivers: "I don't understand why they have sent us Czechs."

He was determined not to let Czechs inhabit his village and quite sternly he told the drivers: "Take them back!" And again he said: "I don't know why they have sent me Czechs?"

Soon the deputy Mayor came to our rescue, as he realised the mistake, which had quite obviously been made. He took us to the youth sports hall. We swept it with branches from shrubs. Then he arranged to have straw delivered by some farmers. He was kindly disposed towards us.

Shortly before Easter we could move into one room in a family house. I managed to get a job in the local sauerkraut factory, and after six months I was offered a job in the local post office. At Easter we all went to church and felt a little like ordinary people again.

Years later I talked to Herr Deinwallner about those times and still full of sympathy he told me:

"Several times I had to pick up deportees in Munich-Allach, and every time I found it extremely hard to find some appropriate words which could possibly sound encouraging. I don't think I succeeded, because there are no words which could possibly offer encouragement to a people who climbed onto the lorries after a horrendous journey, with all their worldly possessions in little bundles."

Ursula Hanke

Gdansk, 20th January 1945. One of the most harrowing reports I have heard so far.

Ursula Hanke was the sister-in-law of Resl Hanke. Ursula, called Ursel by her family and friends, lived with her baby boy of three months in the cellar with her parents, cousins and two other families who had a flat in the house. Danzig was relentlessly bombed by the Russians. Cellars usually served as air-raid shelters in cities.

In summer 1987, I spent a holiday with my family and relations in Ismaning. When I told them that I intended to write about Ismaning before, during and after the war, advice came thick and fast. Whom I should ask about this period, what not to forget, and every person I spoke to advised me to speak to Ursel Hanke. I knew a lot of those stories, as I remembered a lot of them. It was the dates I wanted to know - that's what I thought. I was not prepared for Ursel's story, I simply had no idea.

Here I was, in the summer of 1990, sitting next to her on the comfortable settee in their spacious flat, in Ismaning, in Lindenstrasse, her Husband Kurt sitting on the other side of her. It was a lovely flat, with a window looking across the street and onto a football field. At the back of the flat a balcony invited you to look into the forest with its myriad of birds and other small forest dwellers, such as rabbits and small deer.

While we were sitting on the comfortable settee and I told her of my intention to write a book about the time before, during and after WW2 and that I would like to include her experiences. She looked at me and I saw emotion welling up in her, her husband took her hand. I felt that I had made a mistake and felt guilty. Immediately I apologised and said:

"Ursel, I quite understand, if you find it too painful to talk about it. Perhaps it would be better not to talk about it."

To my surprise, quite slowly she said:

"Don't be sorry, I do want to talk about it. I want to tell you everything, it is important, especially if you want to write about it. Maybe, just maybe, it will help just a little to stop another world war. I shall tell you everything, but it will take a while."

I assured her that I would give her all the time she wanted. Slowly she started.

"On 20th January 1945, we were three families living in the cellar, as Danzig was still being heavily bombed by the Russians. I with my three-month-old baby boy, Jürgen, my parents and cousins and another family who lived in the house. It was a house for several families. We all had rented a flat. People used cellars as air-raid shelters, and as the bombing was almost continuous we lived in the cellars. Running upstairs when there was a lull in the bombing to take small furniture, bedding, and clothes and anything else we needed to live down there. I found it still possible to get some milk for my baby.

Then German soldiers and SS men came with the order to evacuate the town, and set it alight to prevent the city from falling into the hands of the enemy. This was the usual strategy of the Nazis. I pushed my pram and we and all the other families who lived in the houses in our street walked aimlessly around. We were dazed and suddenly ended up in the park, found a place on a bench, sat down and just waited. I thought: We are now waiting for death.

There were so many people. Suddenly I heard some people talking about a large ship in the harbour that was called Wilhelm Gustloff, after some big Nazi I am sure, to take evacuees to the west, only women and children. I desperately tried to secure a place for us on the Gustloff, but alas, as so many others would be refugees, we had to stay behind and cope with our fate.

On the 30th January the Wilhelm Gustloff set sail to save 9000 women and children, but the Russians only saw an opportunity to torpedo a German ship and the 9000 women and children including the crew, lost their lives. But as the Germans were regarded as the enemy it was hardly reported. Those who did report it called it war casualties, as so many others. It was not even called a disaster.

The Russians were already camped on the border of Danzig, and with the use of loudspeakers they asked the German public to trust them, to stay in the city, and not to take flight, all the people would be treated fairly and with respect. Above all there would be plenty of food. Surrender and let us enter without causing any more casualties, if you fight you will all die. After all we had been through it was not surprising that we wanted to believe that. We hungered for peace and the end of bombing. After all, we thought, we had nothing to do with the Nazis, those culprits had left long ago. Hitler did say that the good ones had all died in the fighting and those who were left were only Untermenschen (Subhumans). There was absolutely no reason to help or to defend us, quite the contrary; he had even given the order to destroy the German cities in any case, as they would otherwise fall into enemy hands. The enemy should find nothing but cities in ruins. And indeed that was what we found. We went back into our ruined house and again lived in the cellar.

After the Russians made their promises of peace and food, we gladly hung white cloths out of the windows or rather, the holes where there once had been windows. What choice did we have, we had nowhere to go. The bombing still continued. Water became very short; the only place I could get water from was the fire station. I, being the oldest, used to run out between bombing raids to fetch water. Once I was not quick enough when I heard a Stalin's Organ. A German soldier was running in the same direction as I, and when he caught up to me he pulled me to the ground. He saved my life, but he died. I didn't even know his name. Approximately every twenty minutes came an air-raid and in between people left their cellars to get a little water as quickly as they could. Suddenly I remembered that there used to be a water hydrant nearby, so I started looking for it and to my delight found it amongst the rubble and with glee I told some men who managed to open it. Now we had water as much as we wanted. The men also found a wooden hut that was nailed shut. They broke it open thinking there might be food to be had. But they did not expect what they did find. The hut was stacked with dead people, all naked. It was horrific.

Then the Russian troops entered Danzig, and contrary to their promises the first thing they did when they found us in the cellar was to wildly shoot about to frighten us. Then started the rapes. My cousin Irmgard went with them willingly into the adjoining coal bunker, thinking she could save her sister from being raped, for she was still a virgin. But she could not save her sister. All women were raped.

Fifteen soldiers were queuing and this was only the beginning.

Soon afterwards we found accommodation in some barracks, which had been used as a makeshift hospital. Here we received some mattresses, but only a little milk for my baby Jürgen, which I warmed over a candle. Yet life continued in its grim way. Every day the Russian soldiers came to rape us. One of my cousins had tuberculosis, therefore they left her alone for a few days, after those few days they treated her the same as us. After one week the Russians left and the Poles came, but the treatment was no different. Some of the young girls who were with us in the barracks tried to hide one day, then the Poles threatened to shoot all the mothers and children, if the girls wouldn't give themselves up. But they didn't have it too difficult to find the girls. There weren't too many places in the barracks where they could hide. It took those soldiers only a few minutes to find them. Then before raping them, they beat and kicked them. This treatment gave those girls courage and they went straight to the commander-in-chief to show themselves, he asked them to sit down, but they declined as they preferred to stand, sitting was not exactly comfortable for them. He asked a soldier to bring them a glass of water each and assured them that this would never happen again, and it never did. The two weeks of hell had ended.

Now at least we could start to go out and look for food in the fields, mainly potatoes."

Here Ursel stopped talking for a while. I could see how difficult it was for her to speak. I said nothing at all, I just waited. Her tears were flowing quite freely.

I expected the next story she would tell me would be very difficult for her to talk about, as it took some time for her to collect herself. When she had managed to collect herself somewhat, she continued to talk. In between little sobs she slowly continued.

As the story unfolded I too couldn't hold back my tears.

"I had no news from Kurt, my husband. I couldn't get any milk for my baby. Neither the Russians nor the Poles would give me anything for my baby. The Germans couldn't, they didn't have anything. After a while he stopped crying. Then Jürgen died of hunger typhoid. I took him to the cemetery and buried him myself. A priest saw me and came to say a blessing over my baby."

Ursel never did have any children.

"All the men had been imprisoned by the Russians. My uncle was killed and my father was taken to Graudenz, a town in North Poland. From there he was taken back to a camp in Danzig, where I was permitted to visit him. As I was the oldest in the family I started to take care of them. I had a brother of 7 years-of-age and my sister was 15 years old. We only had potatoes to eat, that we found in the fields. My cousin came with me and sometimes we walked 30 km to find some. Very often the Poles took us from the street to make us work for them. For the work we received no food and needless to say, no money. Three times they caught us and three times we escaped. Mother was always overjoyed when we managed to get home. By now we lived in our house again and did the best we could to make it habitable.

Father was still in the prison camp and had to work hard on very little food. Whenever I visited him I saw that he was thinner and looking ill. As an old man with no food to speak of and being very week meant that he was useless for the Poles. They most certainly didn't want to care for him and released him. At least they didn't shoot him. Father thought that that would happen to him in the end. I was permitted to meet him outside the camp. He was a very old, a completely broken man, but it was wonderful to have him home.

As I was a dressmaker I was lucky enough to start working for Polish women. For one woman I had to modernise a fur coat. When I took the altered coat into the office where she worked she was so impressed that she arranged more work for me. I now had work and earned 350 Zloty per week. I could buy bread and potatoes. A small loaf of bread cost 25 Zloty. They made very sure that they didn't overpay me. Although it was a very small amount of money I received for my work, it was enough to buy some food for the family. Father slowly but surely recovered. Now he could rest and had regular meals, albeit meagre ones, he soon got his strength back. We were a family again.

Without a proper home and little food we were determined to try and go to West Germany. We sold everything we had to the Polish. On December 1945 we received permission to go on the first transport from Danzig to Germany. Under normal circumstances this journey would take six hours. Our journey took one week. We had only the bread that we took with us. Whenever the train stopped we collected snow in tins and warmed them in our hands so that we could have a little water. As the train went through villages, more and more passengers boarded it. They entered with luggage such as blankets and bedding stuffed in rucksacks. Our compartment was crammed with people and their luggage. When it was impossible for more people to come on board, the Polish shot the ones who could not enter the train. December 1945 was bitterly cold and the train was completely devoid of windows, either shattered by bombing raids, or smashed by the Polish. Either way, the temperature on the train was way below zero. Many old people died very quickly, and as the train moved on we heard people moaning from the corridor. Most of them could only moan before they froze to death. The cold was so severe that we stopped feeling anything. All we wanted was to get off this train. After one week we arrived in Pommern, here we had to leave the train. We saw a woman lying in the street begging for help, but we were not permitted to help her, we were herded on. We realised that once again we had been deceived. Our destination was not West Germany. The Polish had quite a different destination in mind for us. Transport was organised for women to be transported to Siberia. Not every woman was selected for this notorious place. To our horror my cousin Irmgard had been chosen to join the train to the East. In her desperation she went to the officer in charge and pleaded with him. She told him that she was a teacher and had absolutely nothing to do with the Nazis, and that she had to look after her two younger brothers. He was moved by her obvious sincerity, and told her that he too was a teacher and gave her permission to go back to her family.

The people not chosen for Siberia were transported to the Isle of Rügen, where another camp was waiting for us and so was Christmas. Christmas? Wasn't that to be joyous? We had forgotten what that was. Yet Christmas quite unobtrusively crept up on us. Warm barracks were waiting for us and we could cook some food. Our Christmas present was potatoes and cabbage with a little butter. The potatoes were plentiful, and cooking was done in tin cans. We were deliriously happy. We could live again.

Sadly not all of us found a new life on the Isle of Rügen. Both of Irmgard's younger brothers fell ill with meningitis and died.

In January 1946 father got a job and with that came an attic flat with three rooms. I knew nothing of my husband Kurt. I knew if he was alive he would be imprisoned somewhere. I went to the Red Cross Office on Rügen to enquire whether they could possibly help me to find him. The staff proved to be extremely kind and understanding and asked me of my husband's last address. But at the same time also told me that I had to be patient, as I was one person amongst a great many who were asking for help to find a relation. I expected that and assured them that I would wait as long as it took. Yet the weeks of waiting proved an almost unbearable trial. Thoughts came racing into my head, fired by my imagination. What would happen if he had been killed at the end of the war? They would never find him. Or if he had been captured by the Russians and shot, I would never know. But all my fears did not come true.

After waiting weeks, which seemed endless to me, a letter came asking me to go to the Red Cross Office. I was told that it was possible that they had found him. The last address I gave them was correct, and that he might be on a minesweeper in Travemünde, in Germany. He was imprisoned by the English army and working on a ship in the Baltic. The Red Cross gave me his address and I was then permitted by the authorities to write to him. He received my letter and wrote back immediately. He was well! It was Christmas all over again. His first question was: How is my son?

Now I had to send him that heartrending news that his son had died and that I had to bury him in Gdansk, which meant that we couldn't even visit his grave.

Then the English Navy gave the ship to the Russian Navy who also took the German prisoners. When Russian Navy officers came on board they offered the German prisoners the option of going with them to Russia and working in their own professions and being treated as civilians. The English officers heard of it and advised the German prisoners against it. It was more a warning than advice. None of the prisoners volunteered. Fortunately no force was used, but the German prisoners had to work with Russian sailors. This was quite an experience. The German prisoners did all the work, and when they threw a cigarette end on the floor the Russian sailors literally threw themselves on it and with the tobacco fillings of the stubs rolled themselves cigarettes. They also liked to drink - anything that was not water. Everything that could be dismantled was exchanged for alcohol. Even the alcohol for the ship's compass became a welcome drink. This experience proved to the German prisoners that their decision not to go to Russia was a wise one.

When I mentioned that I thought it was lucky that they didn't forcibly have to go to Russia, Kurt in his sarcastic humour said:

"The Russian authorities probably thought eventually one of the mines would blow us to kingdom come anyway, but it didn't happen. Though sometimes it came very close to that, especially as we had to do exactly as the drunken sailors told us. It became very dangerous, however hard we worked and tried to avoid accidents. Then we managed to explain to those sailors that if they didn't leave us to work on our own, it wouldn't be only us that got blown up. They would get it too. Then we still had to work just as hard, but they more or less left us to do the job."

"In 1949 Kurt was released and in December of that year we received permission to leave the Isle of Rügen and travelled to Ismaning, to the delight of our relations."

Hannelore McMahon

This is the story of my friend Hannelore McMahon, who as a young lady was conscripted into the German Luftwaffe, and had to flee from the Russian Army.

Hannelore's surname was Pfeffer before her marriage. We met in 1980 in Norfolk, where we both lived, and indeed she still resides there, whereas I moved to Nottingham. We have never lost touch and are to this day good friends. When I mentioned to her that I intended to write about my village before, during and after WW2, she enthusiastically offered to tell me her story about the years she was conscripted into the German Luftwaffe. I thought this was indeed a story worth documenting. Hannelore, always was and still is known by the name Hanne. Here she tells about her dream and the reality that so quickly shattered so many dreams in the years of the German Chancellor, Adolf Hitler. I thought it best for her to tell her story herself.

"I was born in 1926, in Fürstenberg, on the river Weser in Westphalia. As a teenager I had a dream to study and become a dentist. I always had the dream that one day I would go to university. But the Third Reich cut this dream short, very quickly. The Führer needed young people to make Germany a nation to conquer the world. There was no room for a dream of an individual person, when orders had to be obeyed. Instead of becoming a dentist, I, as so many other young people, was enlisted into the Reichs Arbeitsdienst (Work duty for young people). I was now employed as a mothers help, in Fürstenberg. The Arbeitsdienst officially lasted one year, but in 1942, with the war in full swing, the Arbeitsdienst was very often cut short. In my case it lasted only six months before I was sent to Gütersloh, in North-Rhein Westphalia, to train to become a telephonist, but after only three months since completing my training the authorities thought that I could be of more use working for the German Luftwaffe. The next thing I knew was that I was conscripted into the German Luftwaffe and was sent to the Finow airfield, near Eberswalde, in North Germany, near Berlin. Here I was trained with two other girls to become

216

telex operators for communication. We had to arrange to receive the necessary spare parts for the fighter planes. We worked there until May 1945 when the Russian troops entered Berlin. The job for us girls had effectively come to an end. But we didn't dare shut down the office, as the SS would not have tolerated this. There was nothing left for us to do but to wait. Yet a kind officer remembered us and telephoned to tell us to take our belongings and leave immediately, and try to go west to find the English troops. We took our belongings consisting of a handbag and an army blanket and left the office. To our delight we found a German soldier with a lorry outside the office block, offering to take us and other personnel to a waiting boat on the local river only 12 km from the airfield. The boat was going west, ideal for us girls. Happily we all climbed on to the lorry with the hope that we soon would be on the boat taking us west, to safety. But the street thronged with people pulling carts piled high with their possessions, others pushing bicycles with their belongings. The lorry made slow progress, but we all hoped the boat would wait. Then after 10 km the lorry ran out of fuel and we had to join the throng. When eventually we arrived at the river, the boat had gone. There was nothing for us to do, but do as everybody else did – walk. At first we made good progress, but after walking for several hours we became very hungry and thirsty. Water we were happy to take from brooks and little rivers, but food was harder to come by. The pace of walking slowed down and the hunger literally became painful. The nights were still cold and sleeping under a tree with only a blanket to wrap around us was possible only for an hour or two, then the long trudge to the west continued. During one of those few successful hours of sleep my handbag was stolen. It only contained my identification card, a travelling clock and a little money and a handkerchief. If a thief thought that he or she might have found something valuable they would have been disappointed, but in those days even an empty handbag was worth steeling. Some of the people had some bread, but ignored our hungry looks. After two days of walking and desperately hungry we came across a field of carrots. Liberally we helped ourselves, rubbed them clean with our hands and greedily munched them and took with us as many as we could carry. We did the same with cabbage, but preferred carrots."

When she told me that, after all those years, she smiled and said:

"You have no idea how heavenly raw carrots taste when you haven't had anything to eat for two days."

"After three weeks we arrived dirty and hungry at the aerodrome in Flensburg in the north of Germany, and were received by the squadron of the Luftwaffe Ace, Werner Mölder. He was not there himself, only his squadron. The young pilots had nothing to do but wait for the end of the war. Flensburg was the last outpost to be bombarded by the English, as they tried to destroy the aeroplanes. We, somewhat dishevelled, found a friendly welcome, especially when we told them that we were the girls who got them the spare parts for their fighter planes. We received some food and warm water to wash. After one week we had sufficiently recovered and were eager to continue our walk home. The young pilots advised strongly against it and thought it safer to sit out the war at the aerodrome. Yet we were too eager to get home and didn't want to be captured.

We tried again to go west and came across a camp enclosed by wire fencing. We saw women and children in a peaceful situation and thought perhaps we could stay there for a night or two. All we wanted was a little food and a corner to sleep in. It was a peaceful camp, mainly occupied by Norwegian women who had babies by German Soldiers. The camp leaders to our surprise were English women in English army uniforms. And there came three German girls wandering into their camp. First of all everything was taken off us. I lost my treasured blanket and my two friends had to part with their handbags as well as their blankets. Then followed the delousing in a most humiliating manner, although none of us had lice. The food for the day consisted of cabbage soup. It was cabbage leaves boiled in water without any kind of seasoning, a piece of bread with a little rancid butter and a very thin slice of pork. We thought at least we have a little butter. Rancid butter is better than no butter! On entering the camp we expected some friendly faces and perhaps a warm corner to sleep in. Instead we had to come to realise that we couldn't possibly stay, we simply were on the wrong side.

On the second night we crept outside and with our bare hands we pulled some grass from under the wire fence and as much soil as we could. As it was not barbed wire we could use our hands. After scratching as much soil and grass away as we could, we tried to lift the fence, and after a while became successful and by pulling and pushing each other we managed to creep underneath and escape.

This experience really frightened us. Now we started walking back again to the aerodrome. The pilots were glad and relieved to see us safely back. Then food was running out once again. The pilots knew something had to be done to avoid going hungry. They stripped the planes of everything that might come in useful for bartering. Flensburg is situated near the Danish border, and the Danes were happy to barter with the pilots. They were especially keen to receive the leather from the seats of the planes and in return they gave fish and vegetables. While at the aerodrome, we saw goods trains coming from the west, piled up high with coal. We thought those trains must come from the Ruhr district. They continued going to the harbour in Flensburg and the coal was loaded onto ships. Where the ships were destined for, we could never find out, but we noticed on the way back the empty goods trains stopped at the train station in Flensburg. We thought that this would be a perfect way to travel back to Westphalia. The pilots didn't think that this was a good idea, they felt somewhat responsible for us. But they so well understood that this was a way for us to go home. We tried to negotiate with the men working at the train station, telling them that we wanted a lift on the empty goods train going back to the Ruhr district. The workmen at the Train station wanted to be paid, but we had nothing left. We had even lost our army blankets at the camp. But the pilots came up trumps again, and gave the workmen some money. Then it was good-bye to the pilots, who wished us well and vice versa.

Once on the goods train all we had to do was watch for the towns and villages as the wagons passed through. We noticed that the goods train only stopped at the larger towns, but slowed right down through the stations in smaller towns and villages. We didn't pay any attention to the coal dust, which the wind swirled around us. We even sat down in it. We were on our way home and that was all that mattered. At first we did try to wipe some of the coal dust from the floor with our hands before sitting down, but it was useless to try. We realised that a coal wagon without a roof cannot be cleaned, the dust could not be shifted, with the wind blowing through every slit of the wagon. There was nothing for it but let the wind have its fun.

As the wagons rolled passed the towns and slowed down considerably before entering a station, one by one my friends jumped off the wagon when the train passed near their home. This proved very successful. I was the last one, as I had to go furthest. I had to wait until the train slowed down coming into Herne. That was where my mother and grandmother with my younger sister lived. I jumped off just before the train entered the station of Herne, a small town near Recklinghausen, in Westfalen. It was going well, I was home, and nobody and nothing could stop me now. In approximately one hour I would knock on my grandmother's door. My mother and younger sister lived with my grandmother as our family house had been bombed. Soon I would join them and this time for good.

On a September night, at 10 o'clock, I walked down the main street of Herne looking like a chimney sweep and didn't care. I thought the first person I see will get a hug. To my surprise there was no first person and no second. Well, I thought they are all at home in their houses, nice and comfortable, just the same as I will soon be. I arrived at the tram stop and not a person was waiting. I was really puzzled now, and still wondering why I hadn't met anybody, and now nobody was waiting for the tram, which would surely come any minute now. I looked up and down the street, which was completely empty. I knew that there had to be people. I could see light in the windows, when suddenly a young man came racing across the street calling to me:

"What are you doing here?"

In surprise I shouted back: "What do you think I am doing, I am waiting for the tram!"

By then he was right next to me, and very much in a hurry he said:

"There is no tram, don't you know there is a curfew on. If the English come, they are liable to shoot us, come quickly. I live with my mother just across the road."

I, of course, had no idea that Herne or any other town for that matter was occupied. I did what he said and ran with him into the house across the street. It all happened so quickly, I had no time to think. The next thing I knew was that a friendly lady received me and immediately showed me the bathroom. I must have looked a sight! After having had a good wash and some clean clothes, which the lady lent me, although far too large, as I am small of stature and was as thin as a rake, I was very happy to borrow those clothes and felt very comfortable. After some food I went to sleep on the living room sofa. Needless to say on this sofa I slept better than I could remember. The next morning I put on my own shabby clothes, which the lady had cleaned as well as she could. After an emotional farewell I was in the street again, but this time the street was buzzing with people and so was the tram stop. I had only a few minutes to wait until the tram came and took me to Erkenschwick, the small town where my grandmother's house was. From the tram stop I only had to walk a few minutes before I knocked on the door, but there was no answer. I knew that my grandmother was probably sewing and mending for some farmer to get some food. As a dressmaker she was very often called for, but I had no idea where my mother and sister would be. I sat myself down on the doorstep, which I used to do when I was a little girl. I thought to myself, I haven't come very far; I am still sitting on my grandmother's doorstep. It did not take long before a lady with a little girl came towards me, pulling a little handcart. It was my mother with my sister. They came from the forest where they had been gathering wood. My mother could hardly believe her eyes, after not having heard from me for months, there I was sitting on the doorstep and as if to convince herself she kept hugging me and kept saying over and over again: "It's our Hanne! It's our Hanne!" It was a reunion I will treasure all my life."

When Hanne told me about the coal wagons going from the Ruhr district to the Baltic to be transported out of Germany, I knew the reason why Germany was completely out of coal after WW2.

Hanne just after the war

Afterword

On 8th June 1942, Shorsh received the *Verwundeten Abzeichen* (medal for being wounded in action) and on 16th September 1942, the *Ostmedaille* (Eastern Front Medal)

After his completion of college for *Hoch und Tiefbau* (high and low building) he worked, as an engineer for the *Freistaat Bayern, Landesamt* and was responsible for the water supply for Nürnberg and district, until his retirement.

Shorsh died on 14th November 1994.

These are the medals that Toni received:

On 1st June 1942, *E.K. 2 Klasse*, on 9th August 1942 the *Ostmedaille*, 1st June 1942, the *Verwundeten Abzeichen, Schwarz* (there was also the same medal in silver). On 1st September 1944 *Infanterie Sturmabzeichen Silber* (for infantry action) and on 18th August 1945, *Lapplandschild* (for service in Lappland).

Every medal Toni received, he gave away. He did not treasure them and he did not want them. All he ever wanted was to be at home.

Until his retirement he worked for the building firm *Heilitt u. Woerner* (formerly called *Heilmann u. Littmann*) as a Polier (site foreman).

Toni was an artist in his profession. A garden wall was a piece of art. Concrete was something that could be moulded into figurines or pictures to be hung on the wall, of which I have four in my house.

Toni died on 21st February 2001.

Then there was Sepp, our cousin, who had, before WW2, trained in the *Löwenbrau* brewery, in Munich, to become a brewer. When he came back from the war, he went to college and became a master brewer, and worked until his retirement at the *Löwenbrau* brewery, in Munich.

On 9th August 1942, Sepp was awarded the *Ostmedaille*, on 16th June 1943 the *Verwundetenabzeichen,Schwarz* and on 10th August 1944 the *Verwundetenabzeichen Silber*.

Sepp died on 28th April 1991, just before his 70th Birthday.

The descendants of these three Soldiers still live in the village of Ismaning today.

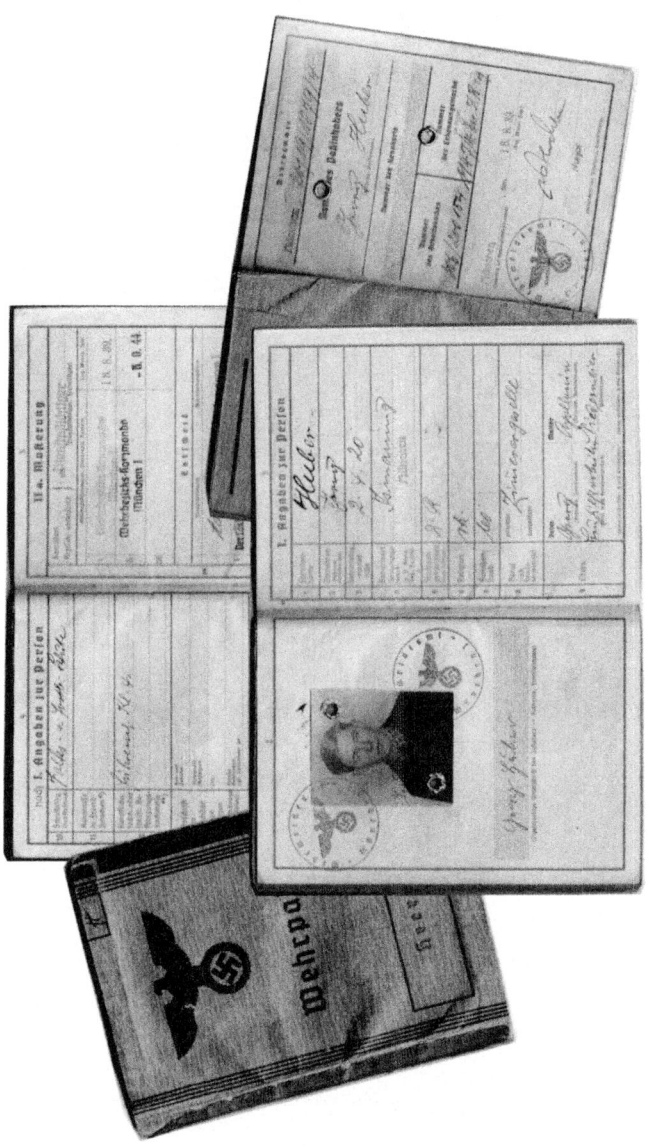

Shorsh's Wehrpass

Toni's Wehrpass

Thomas Diehm, grandson of cousin Sepp in South Tyrol
during his military service

*Sepp & Thomas, twin grandsons
of cousin Sepp in South Tyrol*

Printed in Great Britain
by Amazon

37323565R00136